"In this beautiful, thou ⸱ n
Chapman has spoken with ⸱
I was, the woman I am nov ⸱ be.
She sees the wounds that w ⸱ ⸱ ⸱ ⸱ ⸱ ⸱ ⸱ ⸱ ⸱ ⸱ she points to
the only One who can heal t ⸱ ⸱ An invitation to a personal love story that culminates in holiness, these letters
are a book of wisdom. This is the guidebook we need for
holy womanhood, an essential volume that I look forward
to sharing with my four daughters."

ELIZABETH FOSS
Author and Founder, Take Up and Read

"Inspiring, encouraging, and uplifting. These letters are
filled with Emily Stimpson Chapman's typical humor
and down-to-earth style, and yet they are brimming with
wisdom too. Emily shares from the heart about the ups and
downs of life, marriage, motherhood, faith, and friendship
in ways that speak to all of us, wherever we find ourselves
struggling, and let us know we are not alone, we are made
for more, and we are called to do great things."

DANIELLE BEAN
Author of Whisper: Finding God in the Everyday

"With each letter contained in *Letters to Myself from the
End of the World* you will get a glimpse of the sacredness
of another person's heart. This is what I experienced as
I was reading Emily's letters to herself. Emily shares her
heart with the reader and it is a heart full of hope, wisdom,
humor, sadness, honesty, questions, healing, and faith.
There is a simplicity and authenticity in Emily's letters
that is disarming. For twenty years she has wrestled with

substantive issues—suffering, disappointment, mercy, dreams, relationships, and faith. Emily has grappled with these things and come out on the other side. Her letters on what she has learned are inspired, graced. I look forward to her next installment, twenty years from now, to see what else God has taught her."

FR. DAVE PIVONKA, T.O.R.
President of Franciscan University of Steubenville

"I love the format of Emily Stimpson Chapman's book *Letters to Myself from the End of the World*—such a creative way to share her lived wisdom. She invites us on her journey, and her reflections guide us to reflect on how grace has and will guide us in the future. Highly recommended!"

KIMBERLY HAHN
Author, Chosen and Cherished: Biblical Wisdom
for Your Marriage

"Emily's letters provide a healthy dose of both realism and comfort, and I found myself nodding along, laughing, and tearing up as she vulnerably and beautifully offered encouragement. Emily's candor and wit gave me hope and issued challenge after challenge, and I'm grateful for her words and know that others will be too."

KATIE PREJEAN MCGRADY
Author and Host of The Katie McGrady Show *on Sirius XM*

"This is the book that we all need to read at the end of a year that exposed many of our fault lines. You will soak it up like dry earth receiving a spring shower."

ADELE COLLINS
Blogger, Simple Life Musings

Letters to Myself

Emily Stimpson Chapman

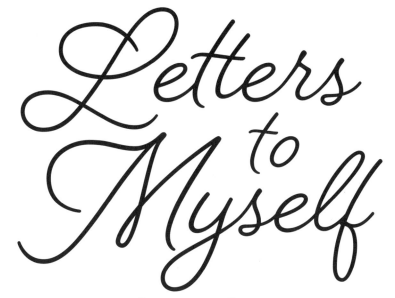

Letters to Myself

from the
End of the World

EMMAUS
ROAD
PUBLISHING
Steubenville, Ohio
www.emmausroad.org

Emmaus Road Publishing
1468 Parkview Circle
Steubenville, Ohio 43952

Library of Congress Control Number 2021936219
ISBN 978-1-64585-133-2 paperback /
978-1-64585-134-9 ebook

Cover design by Emily Demary and Patty Borgman
Layout by Emily Demary
Cover image: *Vintage typewriter and dry flowers front a window* by SianStock

·⁓ⷶ⁓·

For my boys, Toby and Becket.
You are God's joy. And mine.

·⁓ⷶ⁓·

TABLE OF CONTENTS

.ᦿᥱᥣᦿ.

ACKNOWLEDGEMENTS

(and a few notes on how to read this book)

Dear Reader,

The book you're about to read represents one big act of trust on the part of Emmaus Road Publishing. Almost four years ago, in the summer of 2017, I sent them a proposal for a book about my house renovation. It was supposed to be a light, funny memoir about the restoration of the Victorian money pit my husband and I bought after our wedding. Emmaus accepted the proposal. I got ready to write the book. Then, life happened. First, Emmaus had another project they wanted me to do. Then, we adopted our son Toby. After that, Emmaus had yet another project for me. And another. And another.

Finally, in the early spring of 2020, I cleared my calendar and got to work on the book I had proposed. I managed to write two chapters before the world fell apart.

As the Covid-19 pandemic upended life as we knew it, I saw people struggling all around me. They were struggling with the Church. They were struggling with our nation's leaders. And they were struggling with their fellow Catholics on social media. They were also struggling with themselves, with anger, envy, isolation, fear, motherhood, and the normal crosses of life. In them, I saw me. I saw them asking questions I'd asked and fighting battles I'd fought. But they weren't always finding the answers I'd found, answers that have brought me peace and certainty, even in the midst of chaos and confusion. People I cared about were in danger of leaving the Church. Some did leave the Church. Some turned away from Christ altogether.

So, I set aside the book I was supposed to write and started writing letters to my younger self instead. In those letters, I wrote about the questions and battles I've faced since returning to the Church twenty years ago. I shared the answers I've found. I shared whatever wisdom I have to give. After about two weeks of writing the letters, I told Emmaus Road this was the book I had to write in 2020, whether they wanted it or not. Fortunately, they wanted it. They trusted me . . . or humored me. Either way, I am grateful. I'm also grateful for how patiently they waited for the book, through the summer and fall, as our family changed and prepared to change again.

Much thanks, as always, is owed to my husband, Chris, who has done more middle-of-the-night feedings with Becket than I can count these past couple of months so that I could be up at 4 a.m. to finish this book. He also has patiently reviewed drafts of these letters and cheerfully put up with the chaos that inevitably comes when your wife is trying to write a book, mother two babies, keep a house, and get her normal writing done. Whenever I was tempted to burn this book (which I was, many times), he urged me to finish it. So, if after reading it you decide you want to burn it too, blame him for not letting me do it myself and saving you the trouble.

Last, I want to thank my friend Christina, who both reviewed drafts of the book and pretty much camped out at our house during these last few weeks as I've edited, revised, polished, and proofed. Without her help, I never could have squeezed in the extra work hours I needed to wrap this puppy up before spring.

If you've followed me for any length of time on Instagram, some of these letters will sound familiar to you, as a few started out as reflections there and then got expanded upon here. A few more letters have been excerpted there in the months since I first wrote them. Most of the letters were written on or near the dates attributed to them, although in the editing process I have snuck in a few additional letters or done some rearranging for flow and coherency. If any of the letters after July 19 make sense, it's because I went back and edited everything once Becket started sleeping more. If they don't make sense, it's because he's still not sleeping enough.

A few more quick notes before I send this manuscript off to my patient publishers.

First, the letters in this book are short, usually only two to three pages. There are many of them, though, on a range of topics, and packed tight with Scripture, theology, and personal reflections. As such, the book isn't best read all in one sitting . . . or two or three sittings. Rather, it's best read slowly, one letter at a time or (at the most) one section at a time.

Second, although I cover a wide range of topics in these letters, there's more I don't cover. I tried to stick with sins I've struggled with (like anger) and not sins I haven't struggled with (like sloth). So, if I don't write about something, it's not because I don't think it's important. It's either because I don't have any particular experience of it, or because my publishers won't let me publish a five-hundred-page book.

Finally, this book is not a catechetical text. Nor is it a work of fundamental, sacramental, biblical, spiritual, or moral theology. It is exactly what the title says it is: a collection of letters. It is me, sharing my heart, my experience, my knowledge, and my faith with you. It is a gift from one friend to another. It's not meant to be a formal theological treatise, with lots of arguments from authority. It's just me, sometimes explaining Catholic teaching, sometimes talking about the Bible, sometimes handing on practical life lessons I've learned while changing diapers. It's not like any other book I've written. It's not like any other book I probably will write again. So, I hope you can receive it as I wrote it to be received: as letters written for you from a dear friend, who loves you.

All my prayers,
Emily Stimpson Chapman
February 19, 2021
Hawthorne House

Introductory Letters

"JESUS IS NOT YOUR PET."

June 4, 2020
Hawthorne House

Dear Emily,

I think the world is ending. I'm not sure that's the case, having never lived through an apocalypse before. I could be wrong. The actual end could still be centuries or millennia away. Also, if I'm being honest, I expected more fire at the end of the world. Or floods. Locusts, at least. It's possible those things will come later. It's also possible that the only world ending is the world as I've always known it. Either way, right now, the world is filled with pain, confusion, and yelling—a shocking amount of yelling. Especially on social media. Which is a phrase that holds no meaning for you where you are, in the year 2000, so imagine AOL chat rooms, only with pretty pictures and a billion opinionated people who tend to forget their manners.

Anyhow, I'm writing because you've been on my mind these days: myself at twenty-five. You've already been through so much. There's lots more to come though—more good, more bad, more crazy—and almost none of it will go according to your plans. This is hard for you. I understand. We like our plans, you and I. I promise, though, it's better this way. You can't begin to imagine the unexpected beauty the next year of your life will hold, let alone the next twenty years. That's where I am, in 2020. I just turned forty-five a couple months ago. It sounds old, doesn't it? It's starting to feel old, too. Forty-four wasn't so bad. On demographic surveys, I could still check the box for women ages thirty-five to forty-four. Now, I have to check the forty-five to fifty-four box, so I feel like I aged a decade with one birthday.

The birthday itself was less than stellar. We've had a global pandemic paralyzing the planet since early March, with mandated quarantines all through the spring, so we couldn't have a party or see friends or even go out to eat. Instead, I made nachos. It was underwhelming. But easy. And when you're a forty-five-year-old mother of an almost two-year-old, you put a premium on easy.

So, yes, you do become a mother. That's one prayer God answers. It's going to take a while, though. Like another eighteen years. So definitely quit your job in D.C. and go get that graduate degree in theology. You have time.

That's the first piece of advice I have for you. Not the last, though. The world you know isn't the world I know. So much changes. So much breaks. If you're not equipped for the breaking, you will break too. You have some lessons to learn—lessons about sin and grace, about the Church and the world, about friends and enemies, prayer and suffering, motherhood and social media. I want to help. I want to tell you what I wish I'd known about these things when I was you, twenty years ago, newly returned to the Catholic Church and standing on the threshold of a whole new life.

Full disclosure: you can find wiser guides than me. I'm

still learning. I'm still healing. Twenty years doesn't bring as much wisdom as you might think. Fortunately for you, it doesn't bring as many gray hairs either.

We can talk anti-aging secrets another time. For now, just trust that while I don't know it all, what I do know is keeping me sane in the midst of a world gone mad. The air outside is heavy. The darkness is growing. A fundamental shift in how people see each other and treat each other is taking place. And it frightens me.

Inside our home, however, as much as I'm grieving all the hurt in the world, there is joy. There is peace. There is life. Jesus is here. He doesn't change. Which is the best news I can give you. He is the same, yesterday, today, and forever.

The decision you made to follow Jesus is the single best decision you will ever make. Keep looking at Him. Keep talking to Him. Keep listening to Him. Keep following Him. You need Him more than you realize. We all do. He is the One who holds us in existence. Every breath we take, we take because of Him. He doesn't always make sense. He almost never does what we expect Him to do. "He's not a tame lion," remember? That's what C. S. Lewis said about Aslan. But he meant it about Jesus.

Jesus is not your pet. He did not call you to a relationship with Himself so that He could do your bidding. He called you to save you. He called you to transform you. And this transformation won't be a walk in the park.

I'm getting ahead of myself. I'll save the advice for my other letters. My goal is to write forty-five of them, one for each trip I've made around the sun. None will be too long, though, I promise. Thank you for reading them. Every word

I write is a prayer for you. When you read them, please say a prayer for me, too. God is outside of time, so all prayers count.

Blessings,
Emily

2

"THE JOURNEY WILL NOT LOOK LIKE YOU EXPECT IT TO LOOK."

June 5, 2020
Hawthorne House

Dear Emily,

I have so much I want to say to you. I'm not sure where to begin. I think everything will make more sense, though, if you know more about where I am today and what happens in my life when I'm not sitting in front of the computer writing letters to you.

There's a lot of toddler chasing, of course. A fair amount of cooking. More writing, because that's how I've paid the bills for about eighteen years. A little lurking on social media. Then, there's the waiting. Last January, we started the adoption process again, and we've spent the past five months waiting for a new baby.

You know how I said very little in your life goes according to plan, Emily? Well, this is a huge part of it. A late marriage followed by infertility is not on your list of life goals. But that's the story God has for you.

You'll meet your husband, Chris, not long after you turn thirty. He is wise, thoughtful, well read, funny, athletic, faithful, and looks like a J. Crew model. Not surprisingly, you fall hard. From the first, he feels like home. There's only one catch. He doesn't know how he feels about you. Wounds from past relationships, wrongheaded expectations about romance, and a long-term chronic illness complicate his emotions and muddy his thoughts. So, you end up doing the ambiguous friends dance for years. Nine years, one month, and twenty-one days, to be exact. Yes, it is insane. Yes, it nearly drives you mad. But, ultimately, it doesn't. Instead, it drives you to your knees.

In the waiting, in the questioning, in the longing, hurting, and grieving, you fall at the feet of Jesus. When you look up, you see His face in a way you have never seen it before. You see His face on Calvary, black with bruises and red with blood. You see His face broken by those He came to save. You see His face lit with love for those who don't love Him back. It's beautiful. It changes you. It sustains you.

For nine years, you look at Jesus, and He looks at you. That's how you endure. Well, that and a dozen trips to Europe. Plus some pretty dresses. And a lot of dinner parties. But mostly looking at Jesus.

Then, Chris comes to his senses, and life changes. In short order, you go from having a frustrating and complicated friendship to having a wonderful and utterly simple marriage. Being married to Chris is the easiest thing you will ever do. You were right: He is home.

It takes eleven years to get from first date to wedding day, though. You are forty-one years old when you walk down the aisle. Still healthy. Still of an age where babies are possible. But the window is closing fast.

You, being you, know this and do everything you can before your wedding to prep your body for baby bearing.

You visit doctors, have blood work done, and start taking every natural fertility supplement known to man. The doctors assure you that you're still the picture of fertility. They promise a baby will come.

No baby comes. Not after one surgery. Not after two. Not after one round of Femara. Not after six. Not after two years of vitamins, fertility diets, novenas, blessings, and pilgrimages. Not even after you drink some miraculous milk powder from the Holy Land. Your body is broken, your heart is broken, and you feel like a failure as a woman, a wife, and a Catholic. You want to die. The darkness is that black. Those nine years of waiting for Chris? That suffering is nothing compared to this.

You don't die, though. Instead, you remember the face you saw on Calvary—that bruised, bleeding, broken face—and you seek it out once again. When you do, you remember that it's His will you want, not yours. His is perfect. Yours isn't. His is the better one . . . if also the more challenging one. Once you remember that, once you bring yourself to again say, "Not my will, but thine," He makes His will clear to you. There is a child for you, only this child will grow in your heart, not your womb.

You meet that child in July of 2018. His name is Toby. You are there at his birth and every second afterwards. Today, almost two years later, you've never spent more than a few hours away from him. He is your joy and your world. For him, you would carry that cross of infertility all around the world and back again.

Now, today, you . . . I . . . we . . . are waiting for a second baby. It's easier this time, but still not easy. I'm actually starting to wonder if this is what God wants for us. Maybe this is my will, not His. Maybe I'm trying to make something happen that isn't meant to be.

I don't know. I'm confused. But I'm also okay. I would love to hold the warm weight of a little body against me in the night just one more time. After all these years, though, I think I finally trust that God knows best. At the very least, I'm no longer angry at Him for not meeting my desires on my timeline. I'm sad. But I'm not angry. And unlike four years ago or fourteen years ago or twenty-four years ago, I don't feel unheard by Him or unloved by Him simply because I'm unanswered by Him.

When I was you, giving Jesus my heart and coming back to the Catholic Church, I thought I was signing up for a whole different life, a life where I got to be the young bride and the young mom, with a half-dozen redheaded girls who grew in my belly. And deep down, until the day Toby was placed in my arms, a part of me resented God for not saying yes to those plans. After all, they were good ones! Really good ones! It's not like I wanted to be a pole dancer in Vegas. My plans were Catholic and countercultural and full of sacrificial love. Then, when God said no to them, I thought He wasn't loving me. I thought He didn't care. Or that He thought less of me than other women. Like I wasn't good enough for those plans. Like I wasn't good enough to be a mom.

I'd gotten it wrong from the start, though. My return to the Church wasn't about God saying yes to my plans. It wasn't about Him endorsing my idea for what a fruitful and holy life looked like. It was me saying yes to His plans. It was me handing Him the reins of my life. He knew the direction I needed to go. He knew what I most needed to grow closer to Him. It wasn't a marriage at twenty-five or a baby in my belly. It was a marriage at forty-one to a man named Chris and a baby named Toby, who grew in another woman's body but couldn't grow up in her arms.

In time, Emily, you will come to see that this is life for everyone, not just you. We come to Jesus with our tightly held plans, and as soon as we say yes to Him, He starts prying our fingers off those plans, one by one. How He does that looks different for every person, but when you give your life to God, it's inevitable. "These are His ways, unfathomable and incomprehensible to us," wrote the twentieth-century Polish mystic, St. Faustina, in her diary.

She continued, "It is for us to submit ourselves completely to His holy will. There are mysteries that the human mind will never fathom here on earth; eternity will reveal them."[1]

Expect that. If you want to be a saint, expect to be confounded. Expect to be surprised. Expect the journey to look nothing like you thought it would look. Your plans will be upended. The route will have more twists and hills than anticipated. You won't understand what God is doing. You won't see what's coming.

You don't have to see, though. He does. He always has. Before the world was made, God saw it all. Now, in time, He's always there, working through every circumstance in your life to lead you closer to Him.

Don't ever believe God loves you less, Emily, just because life doesn't go according to plan. God is always loving you perfectly, even when it doesn't feel like it. Time will show you this. I promise.

Blessings,
Emily

On Holiness

.ᴐ⌾ᴄ.

3

"GOD MADE YOU FOR MORE."

June 8, 2020

Hawthorne House

Dear Emily,

It's early morning here, just after 4:30. The world is dark, the house is quiet, and I'm sitting here thinking about you. Mostly, I'm thinking I'm glad I'm not you. No offense. It would be nice to have your waistline. And your energy. I could use some of that twenty-five-year-old energy right about now. The month ahead is filled with guests, deadlines, and travel. Not to mention Toby's new favorite game is running away from me. Energy would be lovely. Nevertheless, I wouldn't trade my exhaustion for your insecurities. Not for the world.

I remember you at twenty-five, Emily. You're working in D.C. and already weary of politics. You've just come back to the Catholic Church after five years away. You're whip smart, hypercompetitive, and have the organizational skills to take over a small country. You're also an insecure wreck.

Since you were nineteen, you've struggled with anorexia, and you never feel like you're enough. You think you're not feminine enough, not funny enough, not gentle enough, not good enough. So, you walk around all the time wishing you were different than you are.

You don't need to be different, Emily. You need to be

better, but not different.

You, as God made you, are a wonder. Your intelligence and ideas, your passion about what you believe, your strength, and your willingness to fight for what's right—they are part of who you are. They don't make you less of a woman or a bad woman or the wrong sort of woman. They make you Emily, a unique and unrepeatable image of God. You have to get it out of your head that there is just one way to be a woman. There's not. There are as many ways to be a woman as there are women.

Remember, God is infinite. He is without limit, in Himself and in all His attributes. His intelligence, wisdom, power, beauty, strength, justice, mercy, goodness, creativity—there is neither beginning nor end to them. The seemingly endless differences in His creatures reflect this. We're all made in His image. But even an infinite number of human persons couldn't capture the infinite wonder that is God.

St. Thomas Aquinas posited that every angel is so different from every other angel that you could say each angel is its own species. It's not quite that way with men and women. We are all members of the human race. But we also are each our own, one of a kind, irreplaceable, as singular as the stars in the sky.

Stop thinking you need to be different than you are—that you need to have different gifts, talents, or interests. You are God's masterpiece (see Eph 2:10). No work of art in the Louvre is more well crafted or more loved by its maker than you are by yours.

This doesn't mean, however, that you don't have room for improvement.

You and I both know you're not living as the woman God created you to be, Emily. You may be a masterpiece, but you've made some foolish choices and slapped some muck on yourself, marring the image of God that you are. You've also had some muck slapped on you by others' foolish choices. You're a masterpiece covered in muck. This can't go on.

God has given you so many gifts, and you need to use those gifts better. You need to use your intelligence to serve God, not yourself. You need to express your opinions in a way that is more considerate of others. And you need to control your strength so you can help people with it, rather than roll over them with it. God promises He will never break the bruised reed. He expects you to do the same.

You also need to listen to God and do what He asks you to do. You need to see where you are choosing your will, not His, and start making different choices. You need to see the brokenness inside of you—all the wounds, sins, fears, and disordered desires—and receive the healing graces God wants to give you.

It's okay that you're broken, Emily. Well, not okay. But not unusual either. Everyone is broken. Everyone is falling short. Everyone is more wounded than you can possibly realize. This is the human condition. Forget all the metaphors you've heard about Original Sin being a stain or a mark on us. It's not. It's a hole. As a teacher and friend will tell you someday, "We're born deprived, not depraved." We're all born deprived of sanctifying grace—which is the life of God in our souls.

Because of a terrible choice made by our first parents, we don't have the life in us God meant us to have. And even though Baptism restores that life to us, the effects of Original Sin remain. The Church calls this concupiscence. Which is a fancy way of saying we all have a tendency to sin. We're all weak in some way. And all the crazy that surrounds us—the violence, rage, hatred, cruelty, loneliness, and loss—all that flows from our common human weakness.

Brokenness doesn't have to be the end of our story, though. Jesus offers you a path back to wholeness. He offers you Himself. He is the path. He will make you whole again. He will give you the grace you need to become the woman you are—fully Emily. The same Emily, but a better Emily. The real Emily, I guess.

Don't listen to the voices that say you need to be different—that you need to be less intelligent, less tenacious, less passionate about what is right, true, and good. But do listen to the quiet voice of God telling you that He made you for more.

Until tomorrow.

Blessings,
Emily

"YOU ARE MORE BROKEN THAN YOU KNOW."

June 9, 2020
Hawthorne House

Dear Emily,

Yesterday, we talked about how you need to become better than you are. That doesn't sound all that hard, right? Not for you. You're a hard worker—competitive, responsible, disciplined. Whatever you set your mind to, you usually do. This is different, though. Because you are more broken than you know.

I'm sorry if that sounds harsh. Toby decided to have an all-night party last night, so I'm feeling sharper than normal. But this isn't an attack or a criticism. It's said with the utmost love. At this point in your life, you have no idea of the depths of your wounds. You don't see how deeply you've been hurt, both by your own bad choices and by the words and actions of others. You don't see how much there is in you that needs to be transformed.

You do see some of it. You're not entirely blind to your faults. You see your deep insecurities, your need to always win, your habit of talking too much about yourself and not listening to others. But the work of self-knowledge is like peeling an onion. There are many layers to who we are, and we have to work our way through them slowly, one at a time.

In the years to come, as you stumble and fall, God will show you, layer by layer, the brokenness of your heart. He will speak to you through your mistakes, through the criticisms of others, through the words of priests in the confessional, and in prayer, as you nightly review the day and ask, "Where could I have done better?" In these examinations of conscience (which you should start doing now), God will ask you to look with Him into the darkest corners of your soul and name what lives there: envy, pride, vanity, fear, gluttony, selfishness, and self-hate.

It's a mercy this process of growing in self-knowledge is long and slow. To see it all at once would be too much. We couldn't handle it. Even when we discover the truth bit by bit, it hurts. It changes how we see ourselves.

St. Catherine of Siena defined self-knowledge as knowing that God is "that which is," and we are "that which is not."[2] So, God is God; we are not God. He is the Creator, the source of all love, all life, all goodness, all being. We are His creatures, created out of nothing. No matter how strong, smart, and capable we might be, we're still just creatures. We can do no good apart from God. We can accomplish nothing apart from God. All is grace. To see that clearly is to see ourselves clearly. It's to possess true self-knowledge.

You don't know St. Catherine yet, but she was a mystic and teacher who lived at the end of the fourteenth century, and before her death at age thirty-three, she served as an advisor to popes and kings. She also wrote *The Dialogue*, a spiritual masterpiece that explores the soul's journey to God. In *The Dialogue*, she talks about the importance of self-knowledge and acknowledges the pain of seeing our brokenness.

Because of this, St. Catherine tells us that as we grow in self-knowledge, we will face two temptations. The first is to run from the depths of our brokenness, to stop examining our conscience and decide that we're good enough, whole enough, and strong enough—that we don't need Jesus. The second temptation is to see how wounded we are and despair. This is your temptation, Emily. The devil will take advantage of your struggle with perfectionism and attempt to convince you that your brokenness is too much for God to heal. He wants you to believe that your sins and wounds are beyond God's mercy.

When that happens, you need to look into what Catherine calls "the gentle mirror of God." She explains:

> In the gentle mirror of God, [the soul] sees her own dignity; that through no merit of hers but by His creation she is the image of God. And in the mirror of God's goodness, she sees as well her own unworthiness, the work of her own sin. For just as you can better see the blemish on your face when you look at yourself in the mirror, so that soul who in true self-knowledge rises up with the desire to look at herself in the gentle mirror of God with the eye of understanding sees all the more clearly her own defects because of the purity she sees in Him.[3]

To look into the gentle mirror of God is to look into the eyes of Jesus Christ and see perfect wisdom, perfect goodness, perfect justice, and perfect mercy staring back at you. It's also to see perfect love. In Jesus's eyes, you will see your worth, your dignity, and who you were created to be.

At the same time, as you see your reflection in His eyes, you also will see the contrast between who you are and who you were created to be. You can't justify yourself when you're looking at God. You can't say, "I may be vain, but I'm not as vain as that woman on Instagram." Or, "I may not give much to the poor, but at least I'm not a racist like my neighbor." When God is the standard, all our attempts to justify our sins fall flat. We were made to be like Him, perfect as our Heavenly Father is perfect, and we clearly are not.

Seeing all that, how do you not despair?

You keep looking in those eyes. Because only when you see the greatness of your sins can you see the greatness of His mercy. Only when you see the depths of your betrayal can you see the depths of His love. Only when you see the gentleness in His eyes can you finally learn how to be gentle with yourself. And you need to be gentle. God doesn't want to break you, Emily. He wants to heal you. That's what lies on the other side of self-knowledge: wholeness, which is another way of saying holiness.

This is a lot. I'm sorry. But you have to know who you are. You have to know your littleness and brokenness. Only then can you have compassion for others, who struggle just like you. Only then can you understand how much you need Jesus.

Blessings,
Emily

5

"HEALING TAKES TIME."

June 10, 2020
Hawthorne House

Dear Emily,

The house is full this morning. I've got friends in the attic, their children in the playroom, and more friends sleeping downstairs in the den. We dreamed of weekends like this when we bought this house four years ago. It's actually *why* we bought it. Back then, it had nothing going for it other than its size. The whole thing was in danger of perishing by fire, flood, rain, or a good strong wind. For a while, I wanted to burn it down myself. I managed to restrain myself. Barely. But I managed. Now, I'm glad. It's become home.

Still, it took a lot to get us here, both me and the house, including (and I promise this is relevant, so bear with me) hours and hours scraping thick black paint off the century-old subway tile on the bathroom walls.

I hear you. You're wondering what on God's green earth would possess someone to slap black paint on gleaming white subway tile. I have no explanation other than Original Sin.

Fortunately, this guy lacked basic painting skills. He skipped priming the tile and used the wrong kind of paint. Once I picked up a scraper, it came off in ribbons.

The work was satisfying. Results were immediate. But the bathroom was big, and the tile was everywhere. Some of it wasn't easily reached. As the days stretched on, the work became less fun.

Then, when I went to deal with the grout, it became downright maddening. Unlike the smooth, glassy tile, the grout was rough and pockmarked. The paint burrowed into it, and only released its grip when I attacked it with a razor blade. The results were less immediate, less satisfying. No matter how many hours I spent in that dang bathroom, chiseling away at the paint-covered grout, there was always more work to do. I lost track of how many times I walked out of the bathroom, confident I'd gotten the last of the paint, only to walk back in the next day and discover a whole new patch.

Today, the bathroom looks lovely. If you look closely, though, you will find traces of that old black paint lurking in the recesses of the grout. I don't think it's going anywhere until Jesus comes again. Or until we can afford to gut that bathroom. So, until Jesus comes again.

I'm not telling you this in the hopes that you decide to gut the bathroom from the start. Although you should. Rather, I want you to understand why, twenty years from now—after two decades of prayer, sacraments, and growing in both self-knowledge and knowledge of the Faith—you're still making more than the occasional mess.

You see, it's not just our brokenness we underestimate. We also underestimate the power of sin. The sins committed by us and against us have the power to wound us, change us, and stunt us. Undoing that damage isn't the work of a day; it's the work of a lifetime. Or more. Yes, Confession binds up the wounds sin inflicts on us and restores God's life to us. And yes, forgiving those who hurt us helps bring healing. But true healing—true, deep-down-to-the-core healing—takes time. God doesn't just take away all our pain, all our bad habits of thought and action, all our disordered and sinful desires, with a wave of a magic wand.

Instead, He works slowly, through the decades, to make us new. Day after day, year after year, He feeds us with His Word and His Body. He nudges us along in prayer. He introduces us to the saints as models of virtue. He counsels us through the words of others.

He also asks for our cooperation. He asks us to keep studying His Word and receiving His Body. He asks us to keep coming to Him in prayer. He asks us to do the work of growing in virtue, overcoming old bad habits with good new ones. He asks us to seek out wise counsel. And He asks us to say yes to suffering—both by accepting it with love when it comes unbidden and by taking on small acts of voluntary penance.

However, because God desires our love—which to be love must be freely given—He also lets us say no. God doesn't force us to do the work of growing in holiness. So, most of us don't. We do what I did with the paint: we dive into the work when we first give our hearts to Jesus and then give up when that work grows tedious. That's why you see so many Christians bearing so little fruit. They've stunted their growth by refusing to do the work.

Even with the ones who are doing the work, it's not always obvious. In that regard, I am Example A. I'm still too free with my opinions. I still lose my temper. I still think too much about myself and let deadlines, babies, and laundry distract me from loving people as they need me to love them. New challenges—marriage, motherhood, home renovation projects—always end up illuminating the dark corners of my soul. Decades into this journey, I'm still disappointing myself daily. I'm sure some people look at me, lining up for Communion on Sunday, and think, "If God's grace is so powerful, why hasn't it done more for her?"

It's discouraging. Sometimes, like with that stupid bathroom paint, I feel like giving up. But God hasn't given up on me. He is patient. So, I'm working on being patient too. Both with myself and with everyone else stumbling toward Christ.

Remember God's patience, Emily. Also, remember your limited perspective. When you look at yourself, you don't see all the brokenness in your soul or all the progress toward healing you've made. You're too close to it. And when you're looking at others? You have no idea—no idea how deep their wounds go, no idea how grace is at work, no idea what God has in store for those people. Offer no judgement on the state of others' souls. Only prayers.

Healing takes time. But time, along with grace and work, does wonders. I know they do. Because standing here, looking at you, I can see the long, slow work being done in me. I'm not levitating yet. But I'm not the woman I was twenty years ago either. God is doing something, even if you can't see it. So, keep scraping. The work is worth it.

Blessings,
Emily

6

"HOLINESS DOESN'T REQUIRE PERFECTION FROM FIRST BREATH TO LAST."

June 11, 2020
Hawthorne House

Dear Emily,

You were made to be holy.

"I know," you're thinking. "You've said nothing else since you started writing me these letters."

True. But I haven't said enough. Because I know, when I say "holy," you think "perfect." Not just perfect in Heaven, but perfect always. Or almost always. You think those who wear the crown of glory donned it easily, that after giving their lives to Christ, they turned from sin and never looked back, never stumbled, never fell.

That's not how holiness works, though. That's a trick of the devil. He wants you to think holiness is out of your reach, that no stubborn, strong-willed, opinionated redhead like you could ever be a saint. Fortunately for you, the lives of those saints tell a different story.

The saints were a lot of things. Some were brilliant. Some were simple. Some were gentle. Some were fierce. Some were stubborn as mules, and others docile as lambs. A few seemed utterly ordinary to their friends and neighbors. A lot more struck their friends and neighbors as off-their-rockers weird. But during their lifetimes, as they journeyed closer and closer to Jesus, you know what hardly a one of them was? Perfect.

Almost every man and woman whom we now call "Saint" stumbled and fell on their way to holiness. St. Jerome was so irritable and annoying that he got kicked out of just about every monastery he entered and fired from every position he held within the Church. St. Joan of Arc denied her mission from God under pressure. St. John Paul II made terrible judgement calls about episcopal appointments, putting his trust in the wrong people and unwittingly allowing evil men to rise to power. St. Hildegard of Bingen publicly called for killing heretics. And people answered that call.

Yet, the Church still describes every one of these flawed people as "holy." How is that possible?

It's possible because holiness doesn't require perfection from first breath to last. It requires consecration—the unequivocal gift of self to Jesus.

When Jesus called these men and women to Himself, they said yes. Then, they kept saying yes, in the midst of sickness, suffering, persecution, and failure, handing over more and more of themselves to God until He had all of them—all that they were and all that they had to give.

Most saints messed up multiple times, even as they tried to do God's will. Occasionally, they were too gentle. More often, they were too harsh. Sometimes, they weren't able to completely transcend the evils of their day and got mixed up in unholy crusades or found themselves entangled in political power struggles, inside and outside the Church.

But no matter how often these men and women screwed up, they persevered. They kept saying yes to Jesus. That yes allowed His grace to gradually take hold of every part of them, strengthening them, transforming them, and ever so slowly perfecting them.

That's what you have to do too. If you want to be holy, you have to say yes. You have to hand over to God every part of you and every part of your life. You can't hold anything back. Everything has to be offered—your work, your play, your future, your past, your friendships, your hobbies, your desires, your gifts, your social media accounts, the whole kit and caboodle. Jesus gets it all. That's the only way He can redeem it all.

Most of us don't do this. We think we can keep some part of our life to ourselves: a dream or a desire, a sin or a bad habit, hurts from our past or an identity in which we've found meaning. We say, "No, God. This is mine." And that no echoes through every other part of our life, profaning it, limiting our witness, and limiting our love.

That's you right now, Emily. You say you want to be a saint, but your hands are clasped tight around so many things. You don't want God to interfere with your plans. You've given Him permission to tinker along the margins—to help you become more thoughtful, gentle, and patient—but you still want what you want, and you still define yourself by things that have nothing to do with God: your politics, your eating disorder, the wounds inflicted on you when you were a little girl. You've got to let it all go, Emily. You've got to hand it over to Jesus.

Jesus requires it all. He doesn't ask you to be perfect right this very second. Nor does He ask you to be anyone other than yourself. But He does ask for your whole self. "You can't be half a saint," the wise Little Flower once told a young priest. "You must be a whole saint or no saint at all."[4] I know this sounds scary. I promise it's not. For when you give God your whole self, when you place everything in Jesus's hands, He fulfills your desires and heals your hurts and restores your identity in a way that will leave you wondering what you were so worried about in the first place.

And while you think about that, I have houseguests to feed.

Blessings,
Emily

·~୨ଓୄ·
7
"HOLINESS IS A BATTLE."

June 12, 2020
Hawthorne House

Dear Emily,

At the risk of sounding just a little crazy, I want to talk about the devil today. Not metaphorical demons, like drugs or alcohol or the monkey on your back. But the actual devil. Satan. Lucifer. The Father of Lies. That one. Don't worry, we're not going to talk about exorcisms or possessions or anything scary and dramatic. I just want you to understand that holiness isn't simply a journey; it's also a battle.

In the preface to his book *The Screwtape Letters*, C. S. Lewis wrote:

> There are two equal and opposite errors into which our race can fall about the devils. One is to disbelieve in their existence. The other is to believe, and to feel an excessive and unhealthy interest in them. They themselves are equally pleased by both errors and hail a materialist or a magician with the same delight.[5]

Following Lewis's advice, I never like to give the devil too much attention. Life is short. In the limited time I've

31

got, I'd rather focus on Jesus, who is way more interesting, important, and powerful than some old fallen angel. Also, the devil doesn't deserve much attention.

Popular culture likes to depict Satan as exciting, sexy, alluring—the dark and mysterious fallen angel, who's so much more fascinating than the One who cast him from the heavens. In reality, though, Satan's a bore. He has no goodness in him, no life in him, no love in him. He's obsessed with himself and full of petty hate. He also doesn't have an ounce of creativity in his being. He can't make anything. He can only confuse us about what the Creator has made. Which is mostly what he does.

Yes, demonic possession and oppression are real. Exorcisms are real. Ouija boards, crystals, and Magic 8 balls aren't toys. Satan can be utterly terrifying at times, and meddling with dark objects is a quick path to finding that out. But most of the time, Satan doesn't resort to those methods. He doesn't have to. He can achieve his objectives by far more mundane means. This is what makes him so dangerous.

Satan's dullness, his lack of creativity, his inability to come up with any fundamentally new methods of leading men and women astray, is actually his greatest strength. With most of us, he hides in plain view, whispering the same lies over and over again until they become a normal part of our lives. We don't question them or wonder where they come from. We certainly don't see a malevolent fallen angel as the source of them. And so, taking all those lies for granted, many of us, as Lewis noted, end up dismissing the very idea of an actual devil, choosing instead to think of the devil as a metaphor for fallen humanity's baser instincts and believing that all the world's darkness lies within us.

Neither the Scriptures nor the Church, however, allow for such an interpretation. The Church dogmatically states that Satan is "not an abstraction," but rather "a person . . . the angel who opposes God" (CCC 2851). She also teaches that he was an instrumental part of man's primordial fall, as outlined in the book of Genesis (CCC 397). The prophets Isaiah and Ezekiel, as well as the Book of Revelation, allude to how Satan's opposition began, with his prideful rebellion against God (see Isa 14, Ezek 12, Rev 12). Peter in his Second Letter affirms that other angels chose to follow Satan, not God, and were cast into Hell with him for their sin. And Jesus, who faces Satan in the desert before beginning His public ministry, lays bare the truth of Satan's character to His disciples in John's Gospel, explaining:

> He was a murderer from the beginning, and has nothing to do with the truth, because there is no truth in him. When he lies, he speaks according to his own nature, for he is a liar and the father of lies. (John 8:44)

The exact details of Satan's fall from grace are shrouded by the mists of time and space. What we do know is that before man sinned, angels sinned. We also know the brightest of those angels—a creature of pure light, intelligence, and spirit—led a rebellion against God. He saw man, he saw God's plan for man, he saw God becoming man, and he said no. Angels without number said no with him. And Hell was born. Hell is the Land of No—No, I will not love. No, I will not serve. No, I will not choose God's will over my will.

Make no mistake: Satan wants you in the Land of No, too. His legions of fallen angels want the same. He hates you. They hate you. And just as you have a guardian angel, who walks by your side, working to get you to Heaven, other angels surround you, fallen ones, working to get you to Hell.

In this life, we are all caught up in a great battle between good and evil, God and the devil, angels and demons. Satan cannot win. The victory already belongs to Jesus. But Satan is intent on inflicting as much collateral damage as possible. You are the collateral damage. Satan wants to see you wounded, crippled, and bound by sin. He wants to drag you down to Hell with him, and he wants you dragging others down to Hell with you.

Again, I'm not telling you this to make you afraid. I'm telling you this to make you watchful. The devil is a trickster, and he has been using the same bag of tricks to lead men and women astray since Adam and Eve stumbled out of Eden. The more attuned you become to the lies he tells and how he tells them, the more easily you can avoid his snares.

We'll talk more about some of his favorite lies in letters to come. For now, don't pay him too much mind and keep your eyes fixed on Jesus, who loves you and who claims you as His own. The more you let Jesus renew your mind and heal your soul, the more quickly you'll see through Satan's lies, the more powerful your prayers will become, and the more swiftly you'll travel away from the devil's reach.

Blessings,
Emily

·⸕⸙⸕·
8

"HOLINESS IS NOT A
SELF-HELP PLAN."

June 13, 2020
Hawthorne House

Dear Emily,

The house is still full this morning, and I don't have a lot of time to write. Looking back over these first letters, though, I realize I need to make one more thing clear before moving on.

In 2005, in their book *Soul Searching*, the sociologists Christian Smith and Melinda Lundquist Denton coined the phrase "Moralistic Therapeutic Deism" to describe the overarching spiritual beliefs of Millennial teens. Today, you can apply that phrase to most Americans. Not to me, though. Not to the Church either. I don't want you thinking otherwise.

So, what is Moralistic Therapeutic Deism?

Well, like the name suggests, it's not atheism. Moralistic Therapeutic Deism doesn't deny a god's existence; it affirms it. But the god it affirms is like a grandfatherly therapist in the sky, who wants everyone to be happy on earth and who welcomes all "nice" people unquestionably into Heaven. This god doesn't make demands on us or expect us to be anything other than generically kind. He also doesn't expect us to adhere to any one religion or revealed set of beliefs and practices. Instead, we're free to find whatever "spirituality" works for us. And note: "works for us" doesn't mean "changes us" or "transforms us" or "makes us holy." Rather, it means what affirms us and makes us feel good about ourselves.

Like all heresies, Moralistic Therapeutic Deism is attractive because it contains elements of truth: God does want us to treat each other with kindness. God does want us to know we are loved, that we have value, and that we matter. God does want us to be happy.

But—but, but, but, but, but—that's where the similarities end, because the happiness God wants for us isn't the happiness of the world. His ultimate desire for us is not a big house, a Hallmark movie romance, and plenty of money in the bank. It's not us having everything we want in this life, whenever we want it, with no work, worry, or suffering. It's not really about this life at all. It's about Heaven.

That's the happiness God wants for us. He wants us to experience everlasting happiness, everlasting joy, everlasting peace. He wants us at home forever with Him in Heaven. Which is to say, what He wants for us is holiness.

And holiness doesn't come cheap. Not for you. Not for Him. To make our holiness possible, God entered into time, was born of a woman, grew up in poverty, was rejected by men, persecuted by the ruling powers of the world, and mocked, beaten, and tortured by those He came to save. He then suffocated to death on a cross while nails pierced His hands and feet.

Resurrection followed. But crucifixion came first. It's the same for each of us. If we give ourselves to Jesus, there will be life. But first there has to be death—not just the death of our bodies, but the death of our sin; the death of our disordered desires, habits, and attachments; the death of everything in us that falls short of the glory and beauty given to us by the One who died to save us. And death hurts.

If you are pursuing a relationship with Jesus to be happy, now, in this life, on your terms, you will be disappointed. The ship of lasting happiness in this world sailed long ago, with Adam, Eve, and that cursed piece of fruit. Now, the only lasting happiness to be found is in Heaven. If you want it, you have to do what Jesus said: "If any man would come after me, let him deny himself and take up his cross and follow me" (Matt 16:24). There is no other way. All roads to Heaven pass through Calvary.

Which brings me to another important point you need to remember. This journey? This pursuit of holiness? It's not about you. It's about Him. Holiness isn't something you seek simply because you want to be the best version of yourself. The pursuit of holiness is not a self-help plan or a 12-Step Program for recovering sinners. It's a love story. You will not make it to the end of the journey without love. You will not become holy unless you fall in love with the God who loves you and are willing to give up everything for the chance to spend eternity with Him.

Moralistic Therapeutic Deism preaches a weak god, who gives cheap grace to a self-absorbed people. This is not the Gospel. This is not holiness. All its promises are empty. It can't deliver. This is why everyone who subscribes to it is still miserable and attempting to medicate their misery with sex, drugs, and Amazon Prime (which, I confess, you will love when you're a homebound mom in quarantine.

You won't look to it for salvation, though, which is key).

But, back to my point . . . the hard path to which Jesus calls us? Following in the footsteps of the saints and pursuing the holiness God wants for us? In the end, we discover that's the easier path. Because God's promises aren't empty. He does deliver. He wants holiness for you. Which means holiness is yours for the asking.

In the end, when the world's days are done and judgement comes, only the holy get to be with God. Nobody gets to look on Jesus's face who doesn't belong completely to Him. Nobody will be able to stand in His presence who hasn't let Him enter into every corner of their soul and life. Only those who have allowed God to make them completely His own get to rest in the presence of Perfect Love, Perfect Wisdom, Perfect Justice, and Perfect Mercy.

If you are willing to give God everything, though, He will take everything. He's not going to refuse your gift of self. He will accept it all and transform it all, using your hurting and longing and grieving to bring about healing. He will use every death to lead you to life.

And with that, I'll let the topic of holiness rest for now.

Blessings,
Emily

On the Church

·ᴄᴏʟᴇᴏ·
9

"EXPECT EVERY
BELIEVER TO FALL."

June 15, 2020
Hawthorne House

Dear Emily,

Sometimes—not often, but sometimes—I wish I could see the Catholic Church as you see it now, at age twenty-five. You've only just come back to it after five years away. When you left, you didn't know what you were leaving. Growing up, your formation was . . . lacking. But so was almost everyone's back then. The 1980s will never go down in the history books as a golden age of catechesis.

Regardless, you're now making up for lost time, devouring every classic book on Catholic theology and spirituality you can find, going to Mass daily, making your Confession regularly, and spending hours every week in front of the Blessed Sacrament. You are in love. With Jesus. And with His Church.

In a world where so much seems uncertain, the Church seems as solid as the rock upon which she was built, ancient, unchanging, beautiful in both her sacramental mysteries and doctrinal clarity. The Church is helping you make sense of the world. The sweep of history, the movements of men, the rise and fall of civilizations—it's all coming into focus in a new and sharper way. So is the sweep of your own life and the movements of your heart. The Church's teachings on sin, grace, and the stages of the spiritual life have helped you understand your longings and struggles like no therapy session ever has. In the Church, you have found truth, beauty, and grace, and you want to share it with everyone you know.

I still see what you see. Twenty years later, I look at the Church, and I still think her beautiful. She is my mother. She feeds me. She guides me. She comforts me. I would be lost without her. But I also see more. I see her brokenness.

I see the stains on the Church's bridal gown—the blood and dirt smeared on it by those called to lead and serve her. I see the tears of her children who have been misled, betrayed, used, and raped. I see the sins of her members, the pettiness, cruelty, and casual hate that drives people out of her pews as quickly as cowardly bishops and pedophile priests do. And I suppose, more than anything, I see incompetence and mediocrity—sheer, stupid, incompetence that leaves me scratching my head at how so many foolish people have been allowed onto the Barque of Peter's crew. This, I'm afraid, is what eighteen years of working for the Church will do to you.

Even seeing all that, I still love the Church. But I also have come to expect a great deal of disappointment from those who call her Mother.

The Church, like God, is One: She is the mystical Body of Christ. And as the mystical Body of Christ, she is perfect, breathtaking in her beauty and holiness.

The Church, also like God, is Three. She is the Church Triumphant, made up of all the angels and saints in Heaven. She is the Church Suffering, made up of all the holy souls experiencing their final purification in Purgatory. And she is the Church Militant, made up of men and women on earth, working out our salvation with fear and trembling.

It's that Church, the one filled with bishops, priests, and people like you, with which you will struggle. It's the Church Militant that will break your heart.

Will you always be disappointed by the Church on earth? No. Definitely not. Saints are real. They still walk among us. Grace is also real. It is remaking broken souls and bearing fruit all the time. So much good exists in the Church. But you need to be realistic about the human condition. Baptism doesn't erase concupiscence. Holy Orders doesn't magically transform a sinner into a saint. Being made pope doesn't make you perfect. I've said it before; I'll say it again: The journey to holiness is long, hard, and slow. Grace is not a fast-acting formula for anyone.

To complicate matters further, the devil is efficient. He expends the bulk of his energy tempting those whose fall will lead others to fall. It's a dangerous thing to be a priest or bishop. It's almost as dangerous to be a well-known Christian leader, speaker, writer, or even just part of a respected Christian family. The more people who look up to you, the more people whose faith can shatter when your reputation shatters. The devil knows this. He uses it to his advantage.

I don't know why God has arranged things this way. Nor do I know why the graces of the sacraments don't have us all levitating and bilocating instantaneously . . . or at the very least not tearing each other apart on Twitter. It would be so much easier—easier to believe, easier to evangelize, easier to remain faithful.

But God died on a cross to save us. There was nothing

easy about His Passion and Death. So why should our transformation in holiness be quick and painless either?

Regardless, expect every believer, including you, to fall. Expect brokenness. Expect weakness. Expect fear, anxiety, and old, ugly, unhealed wounds that fester and corrupt. Remind yourself that the work of grace is often invisible, that you have no idea what God is doing in people's hearts and minds. You cannot judge His work because you cannot see the bulk of it, which takes place not in front of your eyes but in the hidden corners of the human soul.

And yes, you will encounter nonbelievers who seem kinder, gentler, and more generous than many Christians. When the temptation comes to compare those lovely people to the unlovely people at your parish (which it will), instead wonder at how much holier those nonbelievers would be if they knew Jesus. Perhaps, with Christ, they would be this generation's greatest saints. Also, wonder at how much worse those broken believers would be if not for the grace working within them, keeping greater evils at bay.

As for your priests and bishops, Dorothy Day summed up my feelings nicely:

> As a convert, I never expected much of bishops. In all history, popes and bishops and father abbots seem to have been blind and power-loving and greedy. I never expected leadership from them. It is the saints that keep appearing all through history who keep things going. What I do expect is the bread of life and down through the ages there is that continuity.[6]

Don't put anyone in a collar on a pedestal, Emily. Every one of them is a broken human being just like you. And, unfortunately for them, the standard by which they will be judged is not the one by which you will be judged. Plus, their judgement involves millstones. God loves every single one of them, though—the weak, the cowardly, the heretical, the tired, the proud, the vain, the malformed, the disordered, the malicious, the criminal. He created them. He called them. He died for them. And He wants every one of them to be with Him in Heaven.

The graces of ordination and the prayers of the faithful may be the only way some of those men make it there. So pray for them. But don't put your faith in them. That goes to Jesus alone.

Maybe that's one reason why God allows so many imperfect priests and bishops to lead His Church. To remind us that He alone saves. All grace comes from Him. All goodness comes from Him. He makes the Church beautiful. He makes her holy. He makes her the guardian of truth. So ask Him to fill your heart with love for the Church, even when her children act unlovable. Do that, and you will learn not only to live with disappointment, but to love the Church even more tenderly when disappointments come.

Blessings,
Emily

.꩜.

10

"LOOK TO THE SAINTS."

June 16, 2020
Hawthorne House

Dear Emily,

Last month, someone I respect left the Church. They had all sorts of perfectly rational reasons for their decision, but it boiled down to disappointment: disappointment with Church leaders, disappointment with their fellow Catholics, and ultimately disappointment with God. They expected more of His grace. They thought grace would do more in the world and do it faster. When it didn't, they walked away.

This isn't the first time I've seen this happen. I doubt it will be the last. As I wrote yesterday, when you have a Church filled with broken people, disappointment is inevitable, and for some people, the disappointment becomes too much.

It hasn't been too much for me, though. Not yet. I pray never. But it's possible. It's possible that someday I'll look at Jesus, hanging on the cross, and feel nothing, believe nothing, hear nothing. Faith is a gift we can lose. Each and every one of us. We can't presume we're beyond temptation or won't someday join all those disciples who walked away.

Faith has to be nurtured, Emily. It has to be protected, cared for, and fed. God has entrusted this gift to you. It's pure blessing. You didn't earn it. But you can lose it.

So, why haven't you lost it yet? Why haven't I lost it?

There are a few ways I could answer that question. It's no one thing. But, like that quote from Dorothy Day that I shared in my last letter, a lot of it is that I don't spend much time focusing on bishops and priests. I know wonderful priests and friars, whom I love, trust, and respect. But I don't look to the majority of clergy in this day and age for guidance or encouragement or for an example of how to follow Jesus in this broken, messed-up world. Instead, I look to the saints. I look to Catherine of Siena and Edith Stein, Gianna Beretta Molla and John Paul II, John Henry Newman and Josephine Bakhita, Elizabeth Ann Seton and Pierre Toussaint.

When the Church seems irredeemably broken, Emily, this is how you keep your faith. You look to the saints. When priests, bishops, and popes let you down, you remember the ordinary men and women who became extraordinary by God's grace. Take your inspiration from them. Imitate them. Follow their lead and example. Above all, call on their prayers for the help you need navigating the narrow and rocky path to which Christ has called you.

I know you don't fully understand the Church's teachings on the saints yet. Growing up, the saints weren't anything more to you than marble statues. You didn't know their stories. You didn't know their love for you. Then, you left the Catholic Church and decided the saints weren't just statues; they were an abomination, idols that Catholics put before Christ. Now, you're back in the Church, and you know you're supposed to love the saints, but you're not sure how. They don't look like idols anymore. But they still do look like statues—distant and cold in their perfection, frozen in some long-ago time, out of touch with the problems of twenty-first-century America.

The saints aren't statues, though, Emily. They're real men and women, who, in this world, had quirks and struggles, besetting sins and crippling wounds, sharp senses of humor and (often) even sharper tongues. Yet, despite all that, every one of them said yes to God's grace, unequivocally and unreservedly. Grace then worked wonders in and through them.

Grace still works wonders through them. The saints aren't dead or frozen in time. They are alive—vibrantly, luminously, gloriously alive—and they want to help you be gloriously alive too. Which they can do. As T. S. Eliot wrote in *Four Quartets*, "The communication of the dead is tongued with fire beyond the language of the living."[7]

Let the saints help you. Start making friends with them. Read about them. Sit with them. Ask for their help. In all your needs, great and small, they will never let you down. When you call, they will come in an instant, with no babies or bosses or crises of their own to distract them. They also will never lead you astray. They will be your surest guides through life, with their words and witness telling you more about the way you must walk than any theologian or bishop ever will.

Above all, the saints will remind you that you are never alone. As that old king in Ecclesiastes said, there's nothing new under the sun (1:9). Every problem encountered has been encountered before. Which means someone else has been there. Someone else understands. Someone else knows exactly what help you need to endure. As you will discover, there is a saint for every person, every need, and every occasion: for home repairs and computer crashes, marriage crises and motherhood woes, infertility, loneliness, difficult bosses, more difficult mother-in-laws, doubts about God, and temptations to unbelief. To be Catholic is to know you're walking through life accompanied by legions of heavenly helpers.

And yes, Jesus can and does help us with all our needs, great and small. But His invitation to us isn't just an invitation to Himself. It's an invitation to communion—with the Trinity, with our brothers and sisters on earth, and with every angel and saint gathered round His throne. That communion with heavenly friends deepens much like our communion with earthly friends deepens—through time spent together, life lived together, and help given to one another. When we call upon the saints, we're calling on family, and we're growing in love the way God made us to grow.

Keep your eyes fixed on that family. There is so much darkness in the world. But the light of Christ, blazing in His saints, scatters the darkness. The less you look to the great ones of the world and the more you look to the great ones of Heaven, the more clearly you will see the face of the One for whom you were made, and the stronger your faith will grow.

Blessings,
Emily

"GO TO MASS."

June 17, 2020
Hawthorne House

Dear Emily,

We're in between houseguests, and I don't like it. When the house is full, my attention goes to the guests. When it's empty, my attention goes to the empty bassinet in our bedroom. I'm not sure if God is saying no to this next adoption or not yet. It feels like no.

I'm trying to tell myself that's okay, that what I want is what God wants, and if He wants no baby, then I want no baby. He knows best. His will is perfect. I trust Him.

But I really want another baby.

I feel ridiculous complaining about this. The sky is falling, and I'm worried about an empty bassinet. But a baby is a specific problem I can focus on. I can get my head around it. I can't get my head around what's going on in the world. I don't know what to ask God for. Peace? Justice? Unity? What do those words even mean? Are they actually possible at this point in humanity's blood-soaked story?

I don't know. If they are possible, though, we're going about it all wrong. We're arguing about face masks and looking to an election in November to save us, while at the same time shuttering our churches and making it all but impossible for people to get the sacraments. We've got it so backwards. Because Mass is the key. That's our surest path to peace, justice, and unity. Kneeling before God, present in the Most Blessed Sacrament, laying our sufferings on the altar next to His, receiving His Holy Body into our own, letting the graces of the sacrament transform us, and offering up those graces so they can transform the world—that's how we find our way back to wholeness, as individuals and as a culture.

Make no mistake, Emily: the graces of the Eucharist are real. They are powerful. They are transformative. They are the means by which the Resurrected Christ continues to enter into the world and heal wounded humanity. They are not nice extras to the Faith. They are essential. They are necessary. Jesus told us so.

> So Jesus said to them, "Truly, truly, I say to you, unless you eat the flesh of the Son of man and drink his blood, you have no life in you; he who eats my flesh and drinks my blood has eternal life, and I will raise him up at the last day. For my flesh is food indeed, and my blood is drink indeed. He who eats my flesh and drinks my blood abides in me, and I in him." (John 6:53–56)

The Church, echoing Jesus, teaches the same. She says the Eucharist is the "source and summit" of the Christian life (CCC 2031).

It contains "the whole spiritual good of the Church, namely Christ himself" (CCC 1324).

It is "the efficacious sign and sublime cause of that communion in the divine life and that unity of the People of God by which the Church is kept in being" (CCC 1325).

It is "the culmination both of God's action sanctifying the world in Christ and of the worship men offer to Christ and through him to the Father in the Holy Spirit" (CCC 1325).

And "every time this mystery is celebrated, 'the work of our redemption is carried on' and we 'break the one bread that provides the medicine of immortality, the antidote for death, and the food that makes us live forever in Jesus Christ'" (CCC 1405).

All of which is to say, it's not the man who sits in the Oval Office who will save the world. It's the man whose life you receive on Sunday. It is Jesus, in the Eucharist, working through you to build the Kingdom of God on earth, who alone saves.

There is healing in therapy. There is healing in friendship. There is healing in honest work, virtuous play, just laws, and the love of a good spouse. Chocolate and the occasional dirty martini can help, too. But there can be no true, complete, total, and lasting healing for our broken selves or our broken world without the Eucharist.

You are living proof of this, Emily. Not too long from now, on a gray day in February 2001, you will go to Saturday morning Mass at St. Joseph's on Capitol Hill. You will walk into that church, hating your body and fearing food, just like you have since you were nineteen years old. Forty-two minutes later, you will walk out, thinking your body holy and seeing food as a sign of God's love and a foretaste of the Eucharist. You will never look back.

In a moment, one clear thought about the Eucharist

will do what therapy, prayer, and sheer cussed willpower couldn't. On your way back from Holy Communion, one sentence flashes through your mind: "The most intimate communion I have with God is that I eat Him."

That thought is the fruit of all the reading, all the going to Mass, all the sitting in front of the Blessed Sacrament you're doing right now. And that thought changes your life. Or more accurately, the Eucharist changes your life. That thought just helps you understand why.

What happened to you happens to everyone who goes to God and lets Him feed them, day after day after day. Healing happens.

Frequent reception of and devotion to the Eucharist is another way you hold onto your faith. This is how, in the midst of scandal, apathy, and cowardice, your faith grows stronger. You literally feed it with the Eucharist. Just like your daily bread keeps you physically alive, the Bread from Heaven keeps you spiritually alive. It keeps the life of God alive in you.

The opposite is also true, though. Take away the food our souls need, and sickness follows. "The longer you stay away from Communion, the more your soul will become weak, and in the end you will become dangerously indifferent," St. John Bosco is said to have warned.

Don't let that happen, Emily. Go to Mass as often as you can. Not just on Sundays and holy days, but, when possible, on weekdays, too. This is easy for you now, as a single woman in D.C. But it won't always be. Different seasons will come, putting demands on you that make getting to Mass much less convenient.

When those seasons arrive, remember this: The God of

the Universe wants to be with us so badly and fill us with Himself so completely and animate us so wholly that He takes on the appearance of bread and wine. And He does this not once, but every day, in every Catholic Church, in every country in the world. Every day, Jesus invites broken humanity to kneel before the mystery of the Eucharist and be mystically transported to Calvary. Every day, Jesus invites us to the re-presentation of the one sacrifice that saves. Every day, Jesus invites us to receive Himself in an act of communion so intimate, so holy, so powerful, that the angels bow down in wonder.

So, yes, stay home when you're sick or your baby is sick or snow and ice have covered the roads. Use the prudence God gave you to make good decisions. And don't feel guilty during the years that daily Mass isn't doable because of that baby. At the same time, don't ever let deadlines, sports, exhaustion, or sorrow keep you away from Mass. You need it more than you need anything else in life. The graces, for you and for the world, are worth every sacrifice you make to get there. They are worth the cost. That's why, for two thousand years, from the catacombs to modern-day China, Christians have risked death for the chance to receive the Eucharist. Not spiritually receive. Physically receive. Flesh to flesh. Body consuming Body.

You don't have to risk death to receive the Eucharist. Martyrdom isn't mandatory. Prudence has its role to play, especially during times of plague and pestilence like these. But you need to be willing to risk something for the Eucharist. You need to be willing to sacrifice something. Even if it's just your own convenience.

The graces that will make you, the Church, and the

world whole wait for you in the Eucharist. Don't leave them sitting on the altar.

Blessings,
Emily

"KNOW THE FAITH."

June 18, 2020
Hawthorne House

Dear Emily,

Next week we leave for vacation in Wisconsin, with Mom, Dad, and the whole family. We go to the same house every year, and one of the best things about it is its terrible Internet connection. Between that and the poor cell phone coverage, our weeks there are blissfully quiet. It's like going back in time. You can almost forget how loud the world is. And it is so loud. Everyone has an opinion—about the Church, about the election, about policing, the liturgy, abortion, race, health care, food, vitamin supplements, vaccines, homebirth, floor wax. Really, truly about everything—and they're all shouting those opinions out into a cyber void.

Not me, though. I went silent a few weeks ago. I didn't want to be one more shouting voice. Instead, I'm sharing my thoughts with you. But how do you know you can trust my thoughts? What makes what I say right? Why should you listen to me about matters of the Faith? Other than the fact that I am you, of course.

These are important questions, and if you can't answer them, it will be hard to hold on to your faith in the years ahead. You need to know your faith, Emily. More accurately, you need to know *the* Faith, the Catholic Faith, not someone's opinions about the Faith.

The saints will encourage you in your faith. The Eucharist will nourish your faith. But knowledge will ground your faith. It will anchor it in truth and reason, making it stronger and more sure, so you can withstand the challenges that come at it from the culture and other members of the Body of Christ.

Acquiring this knowledge takes work. It takes a commitment to reading, studying, and thinking through tough questions. It also requires navigating your way through a cacophony of voices, all of whom claim to speak for the Church, but not all of whom do. False teaching and false prophets are everywhere.

To make matters even more confusing, some of those false prophets have real authority in the Church. They are priests, bishops, and religious sisters. If we can't trust them, whom can we trust? Whom can we believe? How can we know what the Church actually teaches if some teachers of the Faith teach error?

This, again, is where you have to do the work. You have to read, think, and pray. You have to stretch your mind, contemplating God and what He has revealed about Himself in Scripture and Tradition. Even if you only have ten minutes a day to devote to studying the Faith, that's better than nothing. It will add up and pay off.

In those ten minutes (or fifteen or thirty or sixty), prioritize Sacred Scripture and the writings of the saints. Read the Word of God directly. Hear His Voice first. Then, read what those closest to Him—His holy ones—have to say about His Word and about Him. Read Teresa of Avila and

John of the Cross. Read Francis de Sales and the letters of Jane de Chantal. Read Hildegard of Bingen, Catherine of Siena, Edith Stein, Thérèse of Lisieux, John Paul II, John Henry Newman, Bonaventure, and Thomas Aquinas. Most important, read the Fathers of the Church: Augustine, Irenaeus, Athanasius, Jerome, Gregory, John Chrysostom, and all four of the Cappadocian Fathers. Immerse yourself in the Tradition. Trust those whom the Church has long trusted.

Next on your list should be Church documents—dogmatic constitutions, papal encyclicals, apostolic letters, and the *Catechism*. I know, Emily, you just finished reading the *Catechism* cover to cover in three weeks . . . while working a full-time job . . . and teaching spinning classes on the side. Oh, to have that energy again! But seriously, that's great. Don't stop. Keep reading. Let the Church speak for herself, without contemporary theologians and journalists telling you what she teaches. In her documents, you will find oceans of truth and wisdom—teachings you never knew existed and which are beautifully and perfectly clear.

After that, read Church history. Read the bad stuff and the good stuff. Read about how the bishops of the Church taught heresy in the fourth century and how the popes of Rome fed the poor in the fifth century. Read about the faithful nuns who prayed for the Church in the ninth century, even as Vikings threatened them with rape and death, and read about the unfaithful priests who kept male lovers in the eleventh century. Read about the monks who built hospitals and homes for the poor in the twelfth century, and read about the popes who lived in luxury in France while the people of Rome starved in the fourteenth century.

Read about the Reformation and Counter-Reformation, the evangelization of America and China, the Enlightenment and the Reign of Terror, the popes and bishops who turned a blind eye to the African slave trade, and the saints who stood up to kings, queens, and presidents on behalf of those same slaves.

You will find this reading equal parts depressing and inspiring. But you also will find it strangely consoling. Scandal, heresy, and betrayal are nothing new to the Church. She's seen it all before. Yet she still stands. If that's not the Holy Spirit at work, I don't know what is.

Last but not least, contemporary writers can be good to read. It doesn't have to be all saints and dead bishops. If it were, I'd be out of a job! When you read contemporary writers, though, read them in light of your other reading. Don't trust those who contradict the saints and echo the culture. Don't trust those who traffic in outrage and anger either, making a literal dime every time you click on their sensational headline.

Instead, trust those who teach you how to live what the saints taught and what the Church has always taught, fully and joyfully, now, in this age. Likewise, trust those who teach that truth is truth, that it can't contradict itself, and that while doctrine can develop, that development is always a deepening—a discovery of a new depth to an old truth—never a change from one truth to another.

Look also to the fruit born by those writers (and speakers, scholars, and priests). Does their writing lead people toward the Church or away from the Church? Does their work inspire people to greater devotion to the Eucharist; greater love for the Blessed Mother; greater reverence for the human person; greater knowledge of Sacred Scripture; greater fidelity to the Magisterium; greater dependence on the angels and saints; greater joy even in suffering; greater willingness to sacrifice; greater obedience to God's commandments; greater generosity to the poor; greater openness to life; greater mercy for one's enemies; and most of all, a greater commitment to following Jesus Christ even in the face of persecution, disappointment, and personal loss?

Jesus told us we would know His disciples by their fruits. He meant that.

I promise, you will save yourself so much frustration and worry if you know the Faith. The more deeply you root yourself in the unchanging truth of the Gospel, the more protected you will be from the confusion which reigns in the world and threatens the Church.

And on that cheery note, I'm off to make beds in the attic before the next round of friends from far away arrive for the weekend.

Blessings,
Emily

·⌒⌒⌒·
I3

"IF YOU WANT THE CHURCH TO BE HOLIER, BECOME HOLIER."

June 19, 2020
Hawthorne House

Dear Emily,

I just looked back on these last few letters about the Church, and I'm worried they're filled with a whole lot of gloom and doom. I'm sorry. That's not my intention. I don't want you to feel like being a Catholic in 2020 is all outrage and confusion. It's not.

So many problems exist within the Church, but so much good exists as well: young priests committed to proclaiming the fullness of the Faith; faithful religious orders bursting at the seams; Catholic colleges rediscovering their mission; parishes flourishing; apostolates growing; families forming. The Church is so much bigger than your diocese or the Vatican or the hierarchy, and when you look beyond the headlines, at real people, striving to live the Gospel, you won't lack for encouragement. I don't. I love being Catholic. I've never regretted my decision to return to the Church for even a moment.

That being said, you still need to prepare for dark days ahead. Soon, in your time, the long Lent of 2002 will begin.

And I can't tell you when it will end, because it hasn't yet. It just goes on and on, with revelations coming out almost monthly about men who were ordained to pastor and shepherd souls, but who danced with the devil instead.

We talked about being disappointed by the Church's leaders earlier this week. In the years ahead, though, you will struggle with emotions that go beyond disappointment. Every time another news story comes out about a priest who hurt children or a bishop who soft peddles the Faith or a cardinal who does . . . worse, you will be angry. You will be outraged. Your choleric, redheaded self will boil over with the injustice of it all.

That's okay. You should feel outraged by these things. They are outrageous. The Church is Christ's Body and Bride. Souls are at stake. Any anger you feel about these things is legitimate.

At the same time, outrage is a dangerous emotion, and you need to be careful about how you express it and what you do with it. Outrage can be addictive. Like all the passions, it gives us a natural high. It fills us with a sense of righteousness and purpose. Which is not a bad thing if the outrage is justified and spurs us on to help right the wrong. That's the purpose of outrage. This doesn't always happen, though. Because outrage is easy and right action is hard. So, the temptation is to linger in the outrage, to cultivate it, indulge it, and keep staring into the darkness, looking for more reasons to feel it.

When we do that, outrage becomes a dangerous force. It can harm others who are wrongly accused by the outrage machine. More fundamentally, it can harm us. If we're not careful, outrage can consume us. It can make us focus so intensely on the problems out there, in the world, in the Church, that we become blind to the problems in our own souls and distracted from the real work God has for us. It also can lead us to commit sins of our own: detraction, calumny, rash judgement, gossip, and scandal.

Beware of indulging your outrage, Emily. When you feel it rise up in you, take it to Jesus. Offer it to Him. Then get on with the work that will actually help this hurting Church: becoming a saint.

Someday, you will write about two remarkable women, St. Catherine of Siena and St. Hildegard of Bingen. Together, they will show you the power of holiness to help heal a scandal-ridden Church. Although they lived two centuries apart, both lived during ages when the papacy was populated by weak, sinful men and when shepherds dressed in velvet while plagues, pirates, and hunger attacked their sheep. You think people are outraged by clerical scandals now? You should have seen them when the whole Vatican up and moved to Avignon for almost a century. Or when schism followed schism and multiple men laid claim to the papacy all at one time.

In the fourteenth century, the people of Rome were so outraged about the pope abandoning them for Avignon that they rioted in the streets. The people of Florence were so outraged about the pope taxing them unjustly that they told him where he could stick his royal tiara. People were literally up in arms about the sins of the Church, and that went on for decades. But it was just business as usual at the French Vatican . . . until Catherine showed up.

Importantly, when Catherine showed up, she did not show up with her guns blazing. She wasn't packing outrage.

She was packing holiness.

Catherine also didn't set off for Avignon on some kind of crusade to stick it to Pope Gregory and show him how wrong he was. Catherine didn't want to go to Avignon. She didn't want to go anywhere. She wanted to stay in her room at her parents' house in Siena and spend all day and night chatting with Jesus. That was her one desire in life. But she didn't get the life she wanted. She got the life Jesus wanted for her. That life involved going to Avignon, out of obedience to Jesus *and* obedience to Pope Gregory, who wanted her to help him negotiate a peace with the Florentines.

Catherine's holiness, however, is the reason the pope wanted her help in the first place. Catherine's holiness is what attracted the pope to her, and her holiness is what compelled him to listen to her.

When Gregory looked at Catherine, he saw Jesus. He saw Jesus's love for him, and he saw Jesus's sorrow over the papacy's sins. That transformed Gregory's heart. It gave him the courage to do what he needed to do and leave his beloved France for the chaotic streets of Rome.

Hildegard of Bingen's holiness did something similar for the popes and prelates in her day. Hildegard, a twelfth-century German prioress, composer, healer, and visionary, was not a gentle, sweet lamb whom people looked at and saw Jesus. At least not for most of her eighty-one years. She was often sharp and angry. But that sharpness and anger didn't convince popes and emperors to stop their wrestling matches, nor did it convince corrupt bishops and priests to take their holy vows more seriously. Her sharpness and anger caused more problems than it solved.

When Hildegard made a difference, it was because

of her mystical visions and her willingness to share those visions with the Church, even when she didn't want to. And she often didn't want to.

The visions Hildegard received from God were a source of profound stress for her. They gave her daily anxiety. Which isn't entirely surprising, given that they included multiheaded beasts raping the Church. Also, like Catherine, Hildegard had desires of her own. She wanted to compose her gorgeous music, work in her garden, and boss her nuns into holiness. But, again, we don't get to pick our path to holiness; God does that. So, Hildegard kept saying yes to receiving and communicating some mighty scary apocalyptic visions, which ultimately put the fear of God into the Church's hierarchy. Her obedience made her holy. It made others holy as well.

Holiness is the best possible response to the scandals in the Church today, too. You don't have to bear the stigmata or have terrifying apocalyptic visions. You just have to say yes to God. You have to do the work He gives you and follow the path He lays out for you.

Like for Catherine and Hildegard, that path won't look like you want it to look. It will involve suffering. It will involve annoyances. It will involve months of sleepless nights, a million loads of laundry, and picking up one hundred small trucks and construction vehicles daily. But following that path will bear infinitely greater fruit than joining into the cacophony of outrage in the culture. The world doesn't need one more outraged Catholic. It needs one more saint.

Give the world what it needs, Emily. Dig your roots deep in Scripture, Tradition, and the writings of the saints.

Cultivate charity instead of anger, wonder instead of cynicism, gratitude instead of bitterness. Serve the poor. Befriend the friendless. Counsel the doubtful. Struggle against the times, leading a life of radical fidelity, humility, chastity, and generosity.

You are the Church, too, Emily. It's a terrible cliché, misused by many, but it's still true. If you want the Church on earth to be holier, become holier yourself. If you want the Church on earth to do some good work, do the work yourself. If you want the Church to be more faithful, become more faithful yourself. Do what you can do. Do what God is asking you to do. And trust He will remain true to His word: the gates of Hell will not prevail.

Blessings,
Emily

"LOOK TO MARY."

June 20, 2020
Hawthorne House

Dear Emily,

I wasn't going to write this morning, as Toby's godparents and their four girls are still here with us, and we have a day full of plans. I didn't want to close out this particular series of letters, however, without a word about the Blessed Mother.

I know, even now, after your return to the Church, Mary remains a sticking point for you. Your struggle isn't intellectual. You accept the four Marian dogmas. You believe Jesus redeemed His mother at the moment of her conception, that God, who exists outside of time, applied the graces of Calvary to her at the first second of her existence, making Mary "full of grace" from the start. You agree that she should be called the Mother of God. She is the mother of Jesus, after all, and Jesus is God, one of the three Divine Persons of the Trinity. There isn't a human Jesus and a Divine Jesus. There is one Jesus. She is His mother.

You also accept Mary's Perpetual Virginity, although you do that more on faith at this point. After you read John Paul II's *Theology of the Body*, however, you'll grasp this dogma with your reason, too. Once you understand that "the body expresses the person," it makes sense to you that Mary's body should perfectly express who she was, a woman fully consecrated to God, completely the Lord's own. As for the Assumption, we all will be resurrected one day, in body and soul. These fragile, fragmented bodies of ours will be made whole. Like Christ's own body, they will be transfigured. So, you understand why Mary, the archetype of humanity, gets to enjoy that grace from the first.

If you and I were sitting together now, you could explain all these dogmas to me almost as well as I just explained them to you. You've read about what the Church teaches, and you accept what the Church teaches. Your head is fine with Mary. It's your heart that struggles. You struggle with her—with who she is . . . or, more accurately, with who you think she is. You know she is supposed to be your mother, model, and guide. You're already praying your Rosary daily. But then you walk into a church and see a statue of her, looking so gentle, meek, and mild, and think, "There's no way I can be like her."

Let's be honest. You also think, "I don't want to be like her." You think being meek and mild means being weak and saccharine sweet. And you know, if you try to your dying day, you will never be that. Mary could model sweetness till the cows come home, but you're still going to be pure redheaded salt. With which you are fine. You prefer it that way. Salt keeps things interesting.

The problem with your normally excellent reasoning, Emily, is that you're looking at Mary as a creature of plaster and paint, not flesh and blood. You're seeing the statue, not the woman.

You won't discover this flaw in your thinking until 2004, when you and a friend head to the theater to see *The*

Passion of the Christ. On the screen, you don't see a statue of a girl. Instead, you see a woman, a grown woman, mature in her beauty and her motherhood, whose face and body both proclaim that she has worked, suffered, and struggled under the weight of her vocation.

Late in the movie, you'll watch that woman move through the crowds, following her Son to Calvary. As she walks, her eyes are fixed on Satan. Satan, who is depicted in the film as a woman—a hideous anti-Mary—stares back. Their eyes are locked on each other. Neither is surprised to see the other. Neither questions the other's presence. They seem to know each other well. Like they are old acquaintances. And Mary is not afraid.

At that moment, you will realize that the real Mary, your mother Mary, stared down the devil, too. She did it not once, but countless times. For Mary's yes to God at the Annunciation was also a no to Satan, a no she spoke every single day. Satan must have thrown every weapon in his arsenal at her. After all, so much of what he wanted— victory over God and man—depended on Mary stumbling, on her saying yes to him and no to God. But she never did. She succeeded where the rest of us fail. And yes, she was full of grace. She had an advantage over everyone else. That gave her strength. But not invincible strength. Eve was "full of grace" too, remember. We know how that turned out.

But Mary said yes. Mary said yes to everything God asked of her. No call went unanswered. No commandment, not even the smallest, went unobeyed. She submitted to Him in all things, regardless of the cost. And there was a cost.

In her heart, the pregnant Mary carried the weight of others' scorn and rash judgement. After Herod's bloody purge left the mothers of Israel weeping for their children, Mary bore the grief of Rachel. She knew the suffering of the oppressed, the refugee, and the stranger when her young family fled to Egypt. She suffered with the whole Church, in every age, as she watched one of the men her Son had called betray Him. On Good Friday, she felt every lash, of whip and tongue, that fell on her Son, enduring with Him the world's greatest injustice. She walked behind Him on the long road to Calvary. On Golgotha, she kept Him company, suffering with Him and for Him. In her arms, at the foot of the cross, she held the body that was given up for us. And then she lived on, helping the early Church make sense of what it meant to be redeemed, of what it meant to be like her.

There was no weakness in Mary. There was gentleness, for she knew how to control her strength, so that, like her Son, she could crush Satan's head, but without breaking the bruised reed. There was meekness (which actually means "teachable," not "cowering"). We know she pondered every moment of her Son's life, receiving every drop of wisdom and understanding the Holy Spirit had to give her.

But there was no weakness. Like any mother, she took on her child's pain as her own. Only her child was the Savior of the World, who bore all the world's sin and all of history's pain. Which means she carried that weight too. Every loss. Every sin. Every fear. Every sorrow. They all weighed on her motherly heart. Yet she did not stumble. She was, without question, the strongest woman who ever lived.

This is the Mary who is your mother, Emily. Lean on her when you feel weak. Look to her when you need direction. Run to her when you lack understanding. When you struggle to love, ask her to share her motherly heart with you. When you struggle to believe, ask for her to share her own perfect faith. When you struggle to forgive, ask her to pour the mercy that abides within her Immaculate Heart into your own. And when those who are supposed to serve the Church shatter your trust, sit with her, who has seen it all before, and ask her to put the pieces back together.

Mary will answer all those prayers and more, Emily. Jesus made you her daughter as He hung dying on the cross. And like every good mother, she takes care of her own. The Church's princes and shepherds will infuriate you. Priests will disappoint you. Theologians will underwhelm you. But Mary will never let you down. She will get you home.

Blessings,
Emily

On Responding to Injustice

15

"LOVE YOUR ENEMIES."

June 22, 2020
Hawthorne House

Dear Emily,

Remember what I said about the end of the world? It's getting worse. I half expect the Four Horsemen to come riding down the street later today.

They might be hard to spot, though. So much else is happening out there. Our country is having a real reckoning with the evil of our racist past, an evil that continues to color our present. But I fear our woundedness as individuals and as a people is preventing us from having the reckoning we need—a reckoning that is healing and life giving, not one that just does more damage. As it is, protestors and counter-protestors have filled the streets for weeks, with the peaceful ones marching, praying, and shutting down cities, and the violent ones burning, looting, and shooting whoever gets in their way. Everyone, on every side, feels angry, and everyone, on every side, feels justified in their anger.

It's the same online. People have staked out their sides—woke or anti-woke, liberal or conservative, Democrat or Republican, secular or religious, pro-mask or anti-mask—and all feel certain that everyone who doesn't agree with them is doing Satan's bidding. So, they attack.

They slander. They mock. They insult.

On the one hand, it's hard to blame people for their anger. Like within the Church, legitimate reasons for anger abound in this country. There is so much injustice. Hurt, grief, confusion, fear, isolation, bigotry, indifference, inequality, poverty, trauma, and loss are everywhere. Of course people feel angry. Of course they want change. There should be change. There needs to be justice.

But the world's ways are not God's ways. And from those who follow Him, He expects something other than burning, shouting, and doxing.

I want to spend the next several letters talking about this. Because you need to know how to navigate both the world's anger and your own in the face of grave injustices. If not, both will swallow you whole. And you won't even realize it. You will be so distracted by your own righteousness, so convinced of the justice of your cause, that you will fail to see the injustices you perpetrate in the name of justice.

This is a normal human failing, but you're particularly susceptible to it, Emily. I blame it on the red hair. And the choleric temperament. You have such a passion for justice. You want to right every wrong, fix every problem, and let no misdeed go unpunished. There is something beautiful about that. But there's also something terrible about it. You have so much compassion for the one sinned against, but for the one doing the sinning, you have almost none. You lack mercy, and so you sin, even while fighting against sin.

Beware of righteous anger, Emily. Be careful of it. Handle it with kid gloves. We already talked a little about this in regard to the Church, but we need to talk about it more. Because righteous anger is a terribly tricky thing. In and of itself, it's not bad. When an injustice occurs, anger is a just response. It's a right reaction. It is, St. Thomas Aquinas tells us, an emotion in accord with reason that can move us to promptly right a wrong.

At the same time, any kind of anger, even righteous anger, is a dangerous emotion. Often, it moves faster than reason. It gets out ahead of our better judgement. When it does that, it can lead us to act rashly and wrongly. For this reason, St. Paul tells just about everyone to whom he writes—the Corinthians, Galatians, Colossians, Ephesians, and Timothy—to "put away" their anger, to let it go, along with bitterness, wrath, quarreling, jealousy, selfishness, slander, gossip, conceit, and disorder. Likewise, St. James instructs, "Let every man be quick to hear, slow to speak, slow to anger, for the anger of man does not work the righteousness of God" (1:19–20).

The anger of man does not work the righteousness of God. Think on that, Emily. And never let anger lead. Even righteous anger. Let it inspire. Let it motivate. Let it move you. But don't let it lead. Don't give it the reins. Those belong to love.

Yes, I know what you're thinking: Jesus got angry. Jesus upended the tables in the Temple. But, my dear, you're not Jesus.

Jesus saw the heart of every moneychanger in Jerusalem. He knew those hearts better than you know your own. Because of that, His judgement of those men and how His actions would affect them was perfect. There was nothing rash about it. There was also nothing unloving about it. Jesus loved those men perfectly. If they were the only people in the world, He would have gone to the cross for them. Perfect knowledge, perfect judgement, and perfect love animated every lash of His whip in the temple. Can you say the same thing about your anger at those who perpetuate injustice?

You need to fight injustice. As a Christian, you have an obligation to help build a more just world. As you do, though, you have to learn to love those against whom you fight. Jesus said so. You must "love your enemies" (Matt 5:44). That wasn't a suggestion. If we don't do it, we can never be like Christ. Jesus died for people who wanted nothing to do with Him, who ignored Him, maligned Him, and sent Him to the cross. Jesus loved His enemies unto death. He commands all who follow Him to do the same.

Obeying this command doesn't require you to have warm, fuzzy feelings for those who are cruel or unjust. What it requires is to desire the very best for those people. Not the world's best, but God's best: peace, love, hope, healing, redemption, Heaven.

It also requires that you see your enemies as persons— not members of a political party, race, ethnic group, class, or religion. Not as "the bad guy" in your personal story either. Instead, see them as an individual person, living a story all their own, with hurts, fears, desires, and worries that have nothing to do with you. They are God's beloved, precious in His eyes, and He is moving Heaven and earth to lead them to Himself. They should be precious in your eyes, too.

You can demonstrate that by showing respect for your enemies. Don't address people in ways that belittle, demean, or dehumanize. Don't speak ill of those who hurt you. Don't seek to damage their reputation as they may have damaged yours. Don't look down on them either, seeing them as less than you, for we all have sinned. We all have fallen short of the glory of God.

Pray for your enemies. Ask God to bless, strengthen, and heal them. Believe the best about them. Give them the benefit of the doubt. And strive to forgive them even when they don't ask for forgiveness. Do as Jesus did, when He hung from a cross, crying out, "Father, forgive them; for they know not what they do" (Luke 23:34).

The world would have had Jesus leap off that cross and overcome His torturers with a mighty show of strength. It would have had Him raise up an army from the stones beneath His feet. It would have had every one of His followers echoing Jesus's own harsh words against the Pharisees, crying out in the streets, "Brood of vipers," "Hypocrites," "White-washed sepulchers."

But that's not what Jesus or His disciples did. It's not what He would have us do either. He knows what the devil wants us to forget—that hate always breeds more hate. It's like pouring water on a gremlin. You think it's going to solve your problem, but instead, you make it worse. Love, however, stops hate. Or slows it. Or changes it. Often, it does it imperceptibly, in ways we can't see. But Jesus sees. He sees the slow working out of every story and knows that, in the end, love saves the day. Or the soul. So, He calls us to love.

Again, this doesn't mean we stand by while others are hurt, oppressed, or killed. It also doesn't mean we hang around in abusive or destructive relationships, letting others take advantage of our love or mercy. We are allowed to feel anger. We are allowed to feel pain. We are allowed to walk away. But, when fighting injustice, we have to fight differently than those who don't know what it means to be loved by Love Himself. (We have to fight with charity, kindness, humility, gentleness, respect, and above all, truth.)

In Christ,
Emily

16

"ASSUME BROKENNESS."

June 23, 2020
Hawthorne House

Dear Emily,

How can you bring yourself to love your enemies? That's what you're wondering, right? How can you want to love someone who doesn't love you? Who, in fact, hates you? Who wants to hurt you or oppress you or destroy you? Or who wants to hurt, oppress, or destroy others?

The easy answer is grace. Grace makes the impossible possible. It's the life of God in us, and it allows us to live in a way that's more than human—that is, in a sense, divine. The more grace we receive—the more we pray, receive the Eucharist, go to Confession, read the Scriptures, sit in Adoration—the easier it becomes to want to love our enemies, to want hate to have no place in our hearts.

As St. Thomas Aquinas so famously taught, though, grace perfects nature. It works in and through who we are. It's not magic. It makes better what's already there. And when it comes to loving our enemies, one of the human qualities that grace perfects is empathy. It elevates the natural human virtue of compassion to a supernatural love. Compassion is not your strong point though, Emily. And it won't be, not until you stop staring so intently at the broken pieces of your own heart and start looking around you, at the broken pieces of others' hearts.

This is hard for you. At twenty-five, you're still focused on your own wounds. Your eating disorder, your struggle with depression, your loneliness, your insecurities—they consume your thoughts. You spend so much time thinking about your hurts, talking about your hurts, and wanting others to understand your hurts that you don't have much time left for thinking, talking, and seeking to understand others' hurts. This will change, though.

You will be single for a long time. Which sounds miserable now, but ultimately brings so many blessings. Among those blessings are your roommates. You will have . . . many. I lost count somewhere around thirty. Anyhow, as the years go by, you will welcome one woman after another into your home—some for weeks, some for years—and the more women who come to stay, the more listening you will do. You'll learn these women's stories. You'll learn that you aren't the only broken, hurting human being on the planet. You'll learn that your brokenness doesn't make you special; it makes you human. Everyone has their wounds. And slowly, you come to see that more often than not, when someone shows the world cruelty, what they're really showing are their wounds. They're showing the world their pain.

If there's anything besides Jesus and grace that makes it possible for you to love your enemies, Emily, it's this knowledge, this experience.

One woman in particular will drive this lesson home. Her name is Ruth. When you first meet her, she is an addict, homeless, and utterly broken, in body and mind. It isn't hard to understand why. When Ruth was just a baby, her parents split. Soon after her eighth birthday, her father was murdered. Four years later, her mother, under the influence of drugs, ran off, leaving Ruth and her older sister to fend for themselves in the ramshackle trailer park where they lived. Ruth was a pretty girl—stunning, actually. And you know what happens to pretty girls left alone in the world.

Everything that could have gone wrong in Ruth's life went wrong—abuse, abandonment, loss. Everyone used her. Everyone betrayed her. Life didn't leave her with one good gift. And it showed. Her brokenness went ahead of her, announcing its presence as soon as she walked into a room. Occasionally, she could be charming. But she was always demanding, trying to control the only things she could control: the light in the room, the temperature of her pizza, the topic of conversation. And when she was really hurt, she raged at the world with whatever she could grab—a baseball bat, a shoe, her fist.

Many of the people fighting in the streets and online remind me of her. Not the peaceful ones, but the violent, most cruel ones. They've been ignored. They've been abandoned. They've been hurt. For some, poverty, inequality, or bigotry are the source of their pain. Others have been hurt by their bosses. Or their parents. Or their fellow Christians.

All that hurt has to come out somehow, and it usually comes out sideways. Some people take the pain inflicted on them by others and direct it back at themselves. They cut themselves, starve themselves, or drug themselves. Others give themselves to people who don't deserve them—people who hurt them—because they don't believe they deserve anything better.

Most people, though, don't hurt themselves quite so

directly. They hurt others. They let their pain make them ugly. It comes out not as a cry for help, but as a racist remark, a fat joke, a rumor maliciously spread, or a knife in the back. The more broken a person is, the more they try to break others. And the more they do that, the more addicted they become to cruelty. It starts to reshape their hearts, making them less like the God who died and more like the angel who fell.

As a mother, one of your biggest fears is that someday your beautiful boy, whom you wanted before you knew of his existence, will hear from some hurting kid that he wasn't wanted. You already hear their taunts in your head. "Your real parents gave you away. They abandoned you. What is wrong with you? Why did no one want you?"

What if he believes them? He could. Because they will target him where they think it will hurt him the most: his adoption.

That's what hurt people do. They strike at our deepest vulnerabilities. And they always know where to find them. Sometimes because it's obvious. But often, I believe, because the devil whispers our weak spots in their ears. Hate finds its mark because the devil directs the shot.

Never be surprised by people's cruelty, Emily. Assume brokenness. Assume pain. Just like you are more broken than you realize, the people you pass on the streets or sit next to in restaurants or work alongside are more broken than you can possibly imagine. When you see a person wrecking the world around them, strive to see not their rage, but their wounds. Then, instead of reacting with anger or hurt, entrust them to Jesus's Sacred Heart.

The more you do this, the easier it will become to love

your enemy. You will still feel anger. You will still feel hurt. But holding the anger back, not letting it lead, and reacting with compassion instead will start to feel more natural, more possible, more not insane.

"More not insane" is a low bar. It's a start, though. Aim for that, and in time, Jesus will give you more. He will give you glimpses into the love that abides within His Sacred Heart. He will give you grace. And grace will take care of the rest.

Blessings,
Emily

17

"BEAR WRONGS PATIENTLY."

June 24, 2020
Hawthorne House

Dear Emily,

I keep thinking about you and how countercultural you think you are: going to Mass every day, praying your Rosary, saving sex for marriage. And you are being countercultural. You're doing some really hard, really good things for the love of Jesus. But the Jews of Jesus's day wouldn't have thought twice about those things you think are so countercultural. Daily worship, daily prayer, chastity—that was the norm back then. That was the norm for most of the past two thousand years.

What did take Jesus's Jewish listeners aback were His instructions to love their enemies, pray for those who persecuted them, and do good to those who hurt them. Now, that was countercultural. It was almost counter-human. It still is.

Jesus's teachings about how His followers should respond to injustice run counter to our deepest instincts. In the years ahead, you will struggle with these teachings far more than you struggle with the Church's teachings on sex or sacraments or anything else. Following them feels, at times, impossibly hard. Following them feels so countercultural that many Christians dismiss them out of hand.

They're just too contrary to our fallen human nature. And none is quite so contrary—or as important—as the one I want to talk about today: bearing wrongs patiently.

If you don't want to end up a crabby, bitter, old woman, you not only need to learn how to react to the injustices you see around you in a helpful, healthy way, but you also need to learn to react to the injustices done to you in a helpful, healthy way. And there will be injustices done to you, Emily. There will be many.

People who have never met you or talked to you will publicly accuse you of faults you don't have and sins you haven't committed. They will envy your blessings while ignoring your crosses. People who do know you, people you once trusted, will tell lies about you, slandering you to avoid taking responsibility for their actions. You will lose jobs twice without cause, once because of the gossip of an insecure coworker, another time because of the fears of an insecure boss. And through it all, nameless strangers on the Internet will send you nasty emails criticizing the length of your hair, the shape of your face, and the choices you make as a wife, mother, and writer.

Then, there will be people who don't mean to do you an injustice, but who hurt you just the same. Like the people who offer you advice about how to get pregnant. ("Have you tried this supplement?" "You should give up gluten." "You just need to relax.") Or the people who respond to the news about your adoption with words like "But don't you want children of your own?" and "Why didn't his real parents want him?"

Some of those people leave you wanting more than justice. They leave you wanting vengeance. Others you will want to correct and reprimand, informing them in no uncertain terms how misguided their words are. Don't they know Toby is your own—as totally and completely your own as any baby you could bear with your body? Don't they know you are his real mother?

At the very least, you'll want to complain on Facebook and get some sympathy.

Don't. Don't complain. Don't correct by saying something cutting. Don't seek vengeance.

If you need to walk away from an unhealthy relationship or an unhealthy place, walk. But do so without committing an injustice in return. If you need to defend yourself, whether privately or publicly, do so firmly but with charity and respect. In your anger, you may not feel like the person who wronged you deserves charity or respect, but not a one of us deserves God's love and mercy, so consider this your way of handing on the grace you've received.

As for the rest, the less said, the better. Sometimes, because certain injustices shouldn't be dignified with a response. Other times, because the words haven't been spoken with malice; well-meaning people frequently say hurtful things. And all the time, because as Christians, we're called to bear wrongs patiently.

Bearing wrongs patiently is the spiritual work of mercy that comes least naturally to you. It's that thirst for justice you have. And again, that red hair. Your hair complicates so many things for you. But our Lord was quite clear on the matter:

> You have heard that it was said, "An eye for an eye and a tooth for a tooth." But I say to you, Do not

resist one who is evil. But if any one strikes you on the right cheek, turn to him the other also; and if any one would sue you and take your coat, let him have your cloak as well; and if any one forces you to go one mile, go with him two miles. (Matt 5:38–41)

Then, there are the Beatitudes. "Blessed are the poor in spirit . . . Blessed are those who mourn . . . Blessed are the meek . . . Blessed are those who are persecuted . . . Blessed are you when men revile you and persecute you and utter all kinds of evil against you . . . Rejoice and be glad, for your reward is great in heaven" (Matt 5:3–12).

It upends the world's logic. It turns everything our culture tells us inside out. At times, it will feel unbearably wrong. But Jesus's words are clear: to be the humiliated one, the rejected one, the persecuted one, is also to be the blessed one. To suffer an injustice is an invitation to solidarity with Him, who suffered every possible injustice along the road to Calvary. To be misunderstood, wrongly judged, unfairly criticized, insulted, mocked, and attacked by an angry mob is a chance to be united with Jesus, who was misunderstood, wrongly judged, unfairly criticized, insulted, mocked, and attacked by the people He died to save.

Don't pity yourself when you're the one who's judged, Emily. Don't nurse feelings of aggrievement or grow bitter in your pain. Instead, curl up in the Sacred Heart of Our Lord. Hide with Him there. Cry with Him there. And wait for the day when all things will be made known, and He will secure perfect justice for you and for all. I know this goes against your natural instincts. I know it's not the world's way. But we've seen where the world's way leads: from hurt to hurt to hurt. This is the way to peace. This is the way to Christ.

Blessings,
Emily

"DON'T PUT YOUR FAITH IN POLITICS."

June 25, 2020
Hawthorne House

Dear Emily,

I sense I'm frustrating you. You look around and see so much injustice in the world. Babies are dying in their mothers' wombs. Children are trapped in abusive homes and failing schools. More and more jobs go overseas, leaving working-class Americans with no way to support their families, while immigrants and refugees are often treated as less than human by the country they thought would save them. Desperate people do desperate things— commit crimes, use drugs, sell themselves on the streets. The justice system all too often plays favorites. And hatred keeps simmering in people's hearts, hatred that takes a concrete shape in racism, sexism, anti-Catholicism, and more.

You see all that, and you want to do something. You want to fix it. That's your nature. And here I am telling you to check your anger, love your enemy, and bear wrongs patiently. It all strikes you as deeply unsatisfying. "God surely can't want us all walking around, turning cheek after cheek," you're thinking. "Doesn't the Church call us to fight for social justice? Isn't that part of the Church's teachings, too?"

It is. But the Church doesn't call us to fight like the world fights. She also sees the end goal differently than the world sees it.

The world approaches its problems like a puzzle. People think if we can gather all the pieces and assemble them together in just the right way, we can fix the problems our culture faces. It believes that if we just think hard enough and work hard enough, we can eliminate poverty, racism, and the cruelty we inflict upon one another.

But Eden is gone, Emily, and it's never coming back. Not until the very end, when Jesus returns to make all things new. When He recreates the world, there will be no poverty, no hate, no murder. There will be no sin. Until then, the poor we will always have with us—the poor in material goods, yes, and also the poor in mercy, the poor in kindness, the poor in gentleness, the poor in compassion, the poor in love. No government program is going to fix the problem of Original Sin. No piece of legislation or ruling from the Supreme Court is going to eradicate the hate that governs so many of our interactions in the world.

This is why the Church's goals are both more transcendent and more circumspect than the world's goals.

The Church's goals are more transcendent because her ultimate desire for men and women isn't economic prosperity; it's holiness. She wants to save souls, not bank accounts. She wants people to know, love, and follow Jesus. She wants us to know, love, and live the truth. Which includes living in the truth of who we are: images of God, possessing an incomparable dignity that must be honored, in ourselves and others.

That knowledge doesn't come to us in a vacuum. It

comes to us in a time and place, and some times and places are more conducive to learning these fundamental truths than others. Accordingly, the Church encourages her children to help create a culture that makes holiness easier, where we're free to become the people God made us to be, and where we receive a taste on earth of the justice we will enjoy in Heaven. The *Compendium of the Social Doctrine of the Church* explains, "Being conformed to Christ and contemplating his face instill in Christians an irrepressible longing for a foretaste in this world, in the context of human relationships, of what will be a reality in the definitive world to come."[8]

The Church wants the world to become a place where justice flourishes, where both God and man are given their due. She longs for a world where all people are treated as the images of God that we are, and she calls all believers to build a culture that reflects the truth about the human person, God, and His creation. These things are good and right in themselves. This is the type of world for which we were made. It also is a springboard to the only place where justice can flourish forever: Heaven.

This is where the circumspect part comes in. The Church has no illusions about the darkness of the fallen human heart. She knows legislation can't fix what ails humanity. Which is why the Church cautions her children against putting their hope in politicians, political programs, or political systems. "As for 'the social question,' we must not be seduced by 'the naive expectation that, faced with the great challenges of our time, we shall find some magic formula,'" cautions the *Compendium*, quoting St. John Paul II's apostolic letter *Novo Millennio Ineunte*. "No, we shall not be saved by a formula but by a Person and the assurance that he gives us."[9]

There always are better ways to run cities, states, and countries. As Christians, we should work to find those ways. Each of us has a duty to advocate for just laws and good public policy. Responsible citizenship is an essential part of Catholic Social Teaching.

As you work for change, though, don't put your faith in politics. Don't expect government to do what it can't. No political leader, party, or ideology will bring you the justice you crave. Only Jesus can do that.

You've worked in Washington, D.C., for over three years now, Emily. In that time, you've watched legislators spin their wheels, making huge trade-offs for small gains, and pursuing the common good only when it serves their self-interest. In so many ways, even the best-intentioned ones are just throwing darts at the wall, guessing about what will and won't make the smallest of differences to the intractable problems of poverty, crime, ignorance, and hate.

Twenty years from now, you will watch your friends who stayed in Washington fight many of the same battles you're fighting now. Many of the same bills are *still* being proposed. The same amendments *still* come up every year during appropriations season. The same speeches *still* get made by the same congressmen on the House Floor. It's like *Groundhog Day*. Only not funny.

As Washington continues to be Washington, the problems we face as a country have grown worse. The rich get richer, the poor get poorer; the prices of televisions drop, but the costs of housing, education, and health care skyrocket; political polarization has us on the verge of civil war; babies are dying in their mother's wombs, but also on the streets of Chicago and New York and in classrooms across America. And don't even get me started on the current pandemic, which has become utterly politicized by everyone in power.

You have no idea how good the year 2000 looks from the vantage point of 2020. At least in some ways. Yet countless people seriously believe an election in November will solve it all.

It won't. It never does. Elections can make some things marginally better, but no change of presidential administrations can fix what ails us now. The laws can only be as good as the people who write and vote for them, and as a people, we're broken. We can't do better until we are better. Our country can't become more just until we, its people, are more just.

Satan must be having a field day. People have cut themselves off from God, from grace, from the sacraments, and the devil has stepped into the vacuum. No law will evict him. No legislation will restrain him. No lobbying effort will silence him when he whispers "Hate" or "Kill" into some mad soul's ear.

But more people going to Mass will. More people receiving the Eucharist will. More people fasting, praying the Rosary, confessing our sins, conquering our temper, forgiving those who've hurt us, loving our enemies, and giving sacrificially to the poor and the stranger—that will indeed keep the devil in check.

Again, do what you need to do on the natural level. Vote. Lobby. March for justice. More important, fight injustice in your immediate neighborhood. Go volunteer at the soup kitchen near your house and actually get to know the people you serve. Offer to babysit for the single mom next door. Give more than you think you can afford to the inner-city church that has just started a jobs program for ex-convicts.

But as you do all that, don't be blind to the spiritual forces and realities at work. Our culture is caught up in a supernatural war, where more than our earthly lives and loves are at stake.

I have a million more thoughts on this, but we're in the middle of a heat wave and if I don't get out and walk now, before 9 a.m., I'm not getting out at all. So, until tomorrow.

Blessings,
Emily

"OFFER REPARATION."

June 26, 2020
Hawthorne House

Dear Emily,

We're packing this morning and getting ready to hit the road for Wisconsin. I don't want to leave for vacation, though, without adding one more thought on responding to injustice.

The brokenness of this earth goes so deep, and the process of its healing is a mystery to me. I know the ultimate answer is Jesus. Jesus came. Jesus died. Jesus rose again. In doing so, He opened the floodgates for God's sanctifying grace to pour into this world once more. I also know one day Jesus will come again and make all things new—a new heaven and a new earth.

But how He does that, how it's possible, how that work of recreating, redeeming, and sanctifying is going on even now as the whole planet seems to be falling apart . . . I got nothing. Or, not much.

What I do know is that Jesus doesn't want to work alone. Even though the graces He won for the world on the cross were superabundant—more than enough to secure our salvation—He still wants all of us who live in Him to work with Him in the redemption of the world. St. Paul was quite explicit about this: "Now I rejoice in my sufferings for your sake, and in my flesh I complete what is lacking in Christ's afflictions for the sake of his body, that is, the Church" (Col 1:24).

God, for reasons all His own, invites us into the work of redemption. He wants us to be a part of everything Jesus did. So, He asks us to lavish love, mercy, and compassion on each other. He asks us to help heal one another. He asks us to pray for one another. He asks us to serve one another. And He asks us to atone for sin—to make spiritual reparation to God for both our sins and the sins of others.

It's that last one—the work of reparation—that catches most people off guard. Yes, we know we're supposed to love one another, serve one another, and forgive one another. But make reparation for one another's sins? How is that possible? After all, isn't that why Jesus had to become man in the first place? Because we weren't capable of atoning for sin on our own?

It's true that if we're operating on our own, with no help from God, we can atone for nothing—not our sins, not others' sins. God has given us so much—including Himself—and every no we utter to Him is a tragedy of cosmic proportions. When it comes to sin, He is always the victim. "Why do the majority of men treat the adorable Savior as if He were their worst enemy?" the seventeenth-century priest St. John Eudes once asked. "How can they be so cruel as to crucify Him every day! Yes, crucify Him; for whoever commits a mortal sin 'crucifies again to himself the Son of God.'"[10]

There's no way any of us can make up for that. Not on our own. But as baptized Christians in a state of grace, we're not on our own. God's life dwells within us. That life makes our prayers, sacrifices, and penances powerful. It makes them efficacious. It unites them to Christ's own atoning sacrifice on Calvary and helps repair the damage inflicted on the world—on the temporal order—by sin.

It's important not to confuse forgiveness and reparation. Forgiveness is what we extend to others when they hurt us. It's a gesture of mercy from the person who has suffered. Reparation, on the other hand, is a gesture of atonement from the person who has inflicted the suffering. It's helping repair what we've broken through our wrong actions.

Think, for example, of boys playing baseball. If one boy throws a ball through a window, the person whose window he broke might forgive him, but the window is still broken. It still needs repairing. The boy can atone for his actions by offering to pay for a new window.

It works the same with relationships. If Chris says something hurtful to me, he can say he's sorry, and I'll forgive him. But the distance he created between us with his hurtful words is still there. Him bringing me flowers or saying something extra kind can help close that distance.

When Jesus died on Calvary, His death atoned for all the wrong men and women ever had done or ever will do. It bridged the gulf created by sin between man and God. But again, because God wants us to partner with Jesus in the redemption of the world, He left room for us to make amends and help repair the damage done in the world by sin.

And so much damage needs repairing.

In America alone, there is massive damage from ongoing sin—damage from the unparalleled horror of the sixty-two million lives lost to abortion since 1973, plus damage from racism, damage from greed, damage from the myriad violations of God's plan for love and marriage (from contraception and premarital sex to pornography, misogyny, human trafficking, and more), plus damage from unjust labor practices, slander, gossip, selfishness, and a billion other sins committed daily.

There is also old damage from old sins that have weakened this country at its foundations. America may have ended slavery a century-and-a-half ago, but the wounds of that horrifying injustice have not closed and have not healed. The same goes for the wounds left by lynching, race riots, Jim Crow laws, institutionalized segregation and discrimination, redlining, and the countless acts of racism committed by individual men and women through the centuries.

As for the Church, we have our own gaping, unhealed wounds from clerical abuse, ecclesial cowardice and cover-ups, pink palaces, rampant heresy, callous indifference, and petty cruelty.

It's easy to sit around and be angry at others for committing those sins. It's easy to point fingers and say, "Look at those terrible people who do those terrible things." It's also easy to tell ourselves that many of those sins were committed long ago, by people we didn't know, and so we bear no responsibility for them, that they have nothing to do with us.

But they have everything to do with us. Every last sin. As human beings, we are one family. We are one people. We fell as a people. We were redeemed as a people. We are our brothers' keepers. By the power of Christ and through the merits of Christ, God invites us to help set the world right. We need to take Him up on that invitation. We need to let go of our anger, overcome our indifference, and offer spiritual reparation to God for our sins and the sins of others.

Offer reparation, Emily. You choose: a daily Rosary, a first Saturday Mass, a Friday fast, a prayer to the Sacred Heart and Immaculate Heart, your middle-of-the-night feedings with a baby, your pain in all the years you'll wait for that baby. Just pick some prayer, penance, or pain you can offer for the sins of your brothers and sisters today and for the sins of your brothers and sisters yesterday.

Offer reparation for the slave traders and slaveholders. For the abortionists. For the pornographers and KKK members. For the pedophile priests and cowardly bishops. For the robber barons and drug lords. For the liars, the cheaters, the slanderers, the adulterers, the murderers. For the people who stood silently by, through it all, doing nothing to stop the injustice being done before their eyes.

We can't build a more just society when the wounds of injustice are still open and bleeding. There has to be spiritual reparation. And if Christians don't offer it, who will?

You want to do something about the injustice you see all around you? This is it. Start here. If you don't, if we don't, it doesn't matter whom you vote for or what you march for or what you post on social media. Without reparation, there can be no healing. And without healing, there can be no justice.

Blessings,
Emily

On the Feminine Genius

"LOVE AS A MOTHER LOVES."

June 28, 2020
Sandy Beach House

Dear Emily,

We survived the twelve-hour drive with a toddler and (after a stopover in Green Bay) have arrived, at last, in Door County.

Mom and Dad started coming here with Annmarie's and Sara's families eleven years ago. I didn't join them until Chris and I were married. I never wanted to do the drive by myself, and there was always so much else going on—deadlines, trips, parties. I regret that now. Those are weeks with Mom and Dad I can never get back. They get old, you know. They get sick. They won't be here forever. I didn't think about that when I was your age. I didn't think about it for a long time. I think about it now, though.

I did not, however, get up hours before the crack of dawn, on my vacation, to write about Mom and Dad. I got up to write about what it means to be a woman.

You're struggling with that question now. You've been struggling with it for a long time, never feeling beautiful enough to be a good woman by the culture's standards, never feeling sweet and gentle enough to be a good woman by the Church's standards.

You need a new measuring stick, Emily. The standards to which you're holding yourself may be how the culture defines femininity or how some Christian sect defines femininity, but they're not how the Catholic Church defines it. Both are caricatures of the true feminine genius.

You will hear this phrase again soon, in a few months, when you stumble into a bookstore near the Catholic University of America and buy an armload of books and documents written by John Paul II. One of those documents will be the pope's *Letter to Women*. In it, John Paul II affirms woman's dignity—that she is man's equal, made in the image of God. He also laments the world's failure (and at times, the Church's failure) to recognize women's dignity, as well as its insistence on reducing a woman to her body and sexual desirability.

When you read John Paul's words, you find peace and the beginning of healing. He helps you see that your intelligence, opinions, and strength don't make you less of a woman. Rather, they're gifts from God, meant to help you love and serve others. The pope also shows you that you don't have to use those gifts like a man would. That's not what God wants. What God wants is for you to use those gifts like a woman. Or, more specifically, like a mother.

Every woman, John Paul II explains, whether she is married or single, fertile or infertile, lay or consecrated, is called to be a mother. Sometimes in body, always in spirit, she is called to love as a mother loves, work as a mother works, live as a mother lives. To do that is to tap into the true "feminine genius."

That needs some explaining. Let me back up.

The Church teaches that "the body expresses the

person." That is, our body makes visible the invisible truths of our soul. It communicates who we are to the world. And what a woman's body declares her to be is a mother. "The mystery of femininity manifests and reveals itself in its full depth through motherhood," John Paul II writes in his *Theology of the Body*.[11]

In other words, just as a woman's body, in both its physical structure and hormonal composition, is designed for physical motherhood—for welcoming, nourishing, and sustaining life within it—so too is a woman's soul. Its natural orientation is to spiritual motherhood—to welcoming, nourishing, and sustaining spiritual life in others. The body bears witness to this. The physical reveals the spiritual, showing us who woman is and what God created her to do. It reveals woman's mission in the world. And that mission is to be a mother—again, sometimes in body, always in spirit.

We live in a fallen world, though. Motherhood doesn't happen for some of us like it should. Not physically. Not spiritually. And so, while some of us have to work to overcome the brokenness of our bodies to become mothers of children, others among us have to work to overcome the brokenness of our spirits to exercise the feminine genius. Actually, most of us do. Because all of us are fallen.

This is triggering a hundred alarm bells in your head, isn't it? Motherhood is a loaded word. And lots of us fear being confined, defined, or limited by it.

But the Church isn't trying to limit anyone when she says women are made to be mothers. She is trying to free us to be who God made us to be and do what God made us to do. Unlike the world, the Church doesn't care if you're a size four or fourteen. If you prefer hiking boots to high heels, she's fine with that. The Church doesn't judge you on the cleanliness of your baseboards, the quality of your cooking, or your inability to operate a sewing machine without cursing like a well-read sailor. She has absolutely no opinions or expectations on any of those fronts.

What the Church cares about is that you love the people God places in your life with a mother's love, spiritually doing the work in the world that mothers do in their homes.

So, you do this when you look at the person in front of you and see in them what a mother sees in her child—a one-of-a-kind wonder, a soul like no other, a glorious image of God, with particular gifts, needs, and struggles.

You also do this when you love the person standing in front of you—when you welcome them into your life, your home, or your workplace; when you nourish and nurture them with attention, wisdom, and encouragement; when you listen to them, comfort them, and help heal the brokenness within them.

And you do this when you teach people, challenge people, serve people, lead people, and call them on to become the person God made them to be.

That's spiritual motherhood. It's loving people tenaciously, sacrificing for them joyfully, and advocating persistently for the little and the least. It's loving others to holiness—prioritizing the person over every other worldly good, seeing the everlasting importance of each individual soul, and helping others to see that too. It's also cultivating maturity, wisdom, and peace within yourself, so that you are free to give yourself and receive what others have to give.

The twentieth-century philosopher, Carmelite nun, and martyr St. Edith Stein described that maturity in one of her lectures on women's education, explaining:

> The soul of a woman must therefore be expansive and open to all human beings; it must be quiet so that no small weak flame will be extinguished by stormy winds; warm so as not to benumb fragile buds; clear so that no vermin will settle in dark corners and recesses; self-contained so that no invasions from without can peril the inner life; empty of itself, in order that extraneous life may have room in it; finally mistress of itself and also of its body so that the entire person is readily at the disposal of every call.[12]

It's that inner disposition—the readiness to see, welcome, and love—that defines the feminine genius. That's the heart of spiritual motherhood. If you're doing that, you're doing spiritual motherhood right. The rest—how you, as an individual, live out that call—will be particular to you. We're all unrepeatable, and how God calls us to live out spiritual motherhood is unique to each of us. We see this in the lives of the saints.

Spiritual mothers can be teachers, like St. Elizabeth Ann Seton. They can be advocates for justice, like Servant of God Thea Bowman. They can be entrepreneurs, like St. Zélie Martin; translators of Sacred Scripture, like St. Paula; and intercessors for the world, like St. Rose of Lima. Spiritual mothers also can be writers, composers, and scientists, like St. Hildegard of Bingen; wise counselors, like St. Julian of Norwich; and leaders of nations, like Bl. Eleanor of Provence.

Part of St. Joan of Arc's spiritual motherhood was providing her troops with the opportunity to go to Confession before she led them into battle. For St. Gianna Beretta Molla, a medical doctor, spiritual motherhood included treating the patients in her care. St. Jeanne Jugan was a spiritual mother when she walked through the streets of Saint-Servan inviting the elderly poor into her home. St. Josephine Bakhita was a spiritual mother when she forgave the men who enslaved her. And Bl. Columba Kang Wan-suk was a spiritual mother when she used her home as a hub for the underground Church in Korea, then endured torture and death rather than betray any of her spiritual children to the authorities.

All these women brought their whole motherly selves to their work, their worship, and their relationships. As they did, they imaged God as only women can and bore witness to God as only women can. That witness didn't limit them. It didn't confine them. It fulfilled them. And it changed the world.

This is what God calls you to do, Emily. This is how He calls you to love. The loneliness and alienation you see all around you in Washington, D.C., will only get worse in the decades to come. Confusion about the most basic things in life—sex, marriage, friendship, human nature—will afflict the entire culture. People will become immersed in a virtual world, where false ideas of beauty and filtered images of reality surround them. Wounded people will wound more people—they will use, abuse, exploit. And people who feel unseen and unheard will let their pain turn to hate.

All these people are crying out for a mother's love. They are desperate for someone to look them in the eye, listen to them, and acknowledge their dignity. But so many women aren't doing this. Or they're struggling to do this. You're struggling to do this. I want to spend the next few letters talking about why. What makes it so hard for you to live the mission God has for you in the world?

Next time.

Blessings,
Emily

·ᕤᘎᕘ·
21

"DON'T ENVY."

July 1, 2020
Sandy Beach House

Dear Emily,

Today, I have a theory I want to share with you. It might be crazy, because it goes against what most of the Church Fathers teach, and to a one they are smarter and holier than I am. At the same time, many weren't what you would call "experts" on the female psyche. Many weren't our biggest fans either. Case in point? St. Augustine.

"I don't see what sort of help woman was created to provide man with, if one excludes procreation," he wrote. "How much more pleasure is it for life and conversation when two friends live together than when a man and a woman cohabitate?"[13]

See what I mean?

Anyhow, seeing as many of the Church Fathers seemed to understand women about as well as I understand mechanical engineering, I think their interpretation of what happened in the Garden of Eden between Eve and the snake is wrong. By and large, they held that pride brought about humanity's downfall. (Pride goes before a fall and all that.) And, for Adam, maybe it was pride. But I don't think Satan tempted Eve to primarily commit the sin of pride. I think, more specifically, he tempted her to envy.

Consider the Serpent's words. "You will not die. For God knows that when you eat of it your eyes will be opened, and you will be like God, knowing good and evil" (Gen 3:4–5).

God had something—knowledge of good and evil—that Eve did not. He possessed. She lacked. And Eve didn't like that. She wanted what God had. She felt, as St. Thomas Aquinas described it, "sorrow for another's good."[14] So, she attempted to take it for herself. Maybe because she thought it would make her happy. Maybe because she thought it would make her wise. Maybe because she thought it would make her like God. Yes, pride is mixed up in that. The two always go together. But mostly, I see Eve doing what women have done every day since Eden: comparing herself to someone else, envying what they have, and sinning in the process.

Now, the Person to whom Eve compared herself was God, which is pretty foolish. We all come up short in comparison to Him. In Eve's defense, however, she lacked options. There were no Instagram influencers with five kids and a lake house hanging out in the Garden. So, she envied what God had, attempted to get what God had, and then tempted Adam to do the same. He did, and that sealed humanity's fate.

Again, my interpretation of Eve's motivations could be wrong. I am speculating. But when I look at her, I see you. And me. And almost every woman I've ever known. Envy is the female sex's besetting sin. We're always comparing. Always noticing what someone else has that we don't. Always wasting so much time and energy resenting that person for what they possess and resenting God for giving it to them: husbands, babies, a big house, a clean house, a successful career, long legs, great hair, more friends, a nice kitchen, good knives. Really, the list is endless. And it's all so silly.

Case in point: you, maybe five years in the future, somewhere around 2005. You will be sitting in church— the 5:15 p.m. daily Mass at St. Peter's in Steubenville. In front of you will sit a girl with the most gorgeous hair: thick, curly, luxuriant—the exact hair you always wanted. And you will spend the whole of Mass not paying attention to the Scripture readings or focusing on Jesus but rather envying that girl for her hair. And then she will get up to go to Communion, and you will see that she has no hands. No hands.

This sounds like a parable. Like something that should be carved on a wooden sign and hung up in some grand-mother's living room. But I swear this will happen. And you will feel like the biggest idiot on the planet for coveting someone's lovely hair instead of giving thanks for what you do have—a beautiful, whole, strong body.

That's what envy does. Envy encourages us to focus on a little slice of another person's life while blinding us to the whole of who they are—what they've experienced, what they love, what they bring to the world. It also blinds us to the good gifts we possess, to the graces we've received, and to the work God is doing in our life. Above all, it tempts us to forget that every one of us is fighting a great battle and, at some point, must carry an unimaginably heavy cross.

From the outside, we know so little of another's per-son's story. We don't see the illness, the childhood trauma, the casual betrayals that took place over the junior high lunch table. We don't see the broken hearts that came before the storybook marriage, the four miscarriages that came before the baby, the parents that divorced, the friend that died, the brutal rape that ripped a life apart behind a locked door in a sophomore dorm room. We see some crosses of some people, but we never see all. Everyone bears secret wounds, even the people we know best. We never really know anyone's whole story in this life. Not even our own. That privilege belongs to God alone.

Likewise, because we don't know the full weight or full number of crosses people carry, we can't know how the blessings or gifts fit into their story. We don't know what's a consolation, what's a grace, or what's actually a cross disguised as a gift. We don't know what God is doing in their life, how much they need what He has entrusted to them, or how great a burden some gifts might be.

Envy is such a silly sin. For there are few lives, if we could see them in full, that we would ever want to exchange for our own.

But envy is also an insidious sin. It weakens the feminine genius, obstructing spiritual motherhood by turning us in on ourselves and eating away at our capacity to see the fullness of the person in front of us. No other sin does such a good job of shattering communion, dividing women from each other, and breeding resentment, bitterness, and cruelty. Envy prevents us from learning from one another and sharing with one another and being enriched by the diversity of gifts and experiences that our blessings and crosses have given to each of us.

Don't envy, Emily. Don't resent anyone for what they have. When that temptation rears its ugly head, say a prayer for the hidden cross that person carries and praise Jesus for every good thing in your life that you can think of, even if it's just the day's first hot cup of coffee. Keep your eyes on what you do have, not on what you don't have. If Eve would have done that, what a different world this might have been.

Blessings,
Emily

22

"DON'T LIVE IN THE FUTURE."

July 4, 2020
Sandy Beach House

Dear Emily,

Today is our last day in Door County. Tonight, we'll watch our neighbors set off fireworks up and down the beach, and tomorrow we'll head home.

I'm not ready to leave. I suppose I never am, but this year it's especially hard. Here, I haven't felt like I'm waiting. I'm just living. In this place, it's easier to rest in the moment. But going home, with the empty bassinet in our room and the infant car seat sitting at the foot of the basement stairs, the old temptation to focus on the future will rear its head again.

Years ago, when I bought my first house, I displayed framed quotes from my favorite books over my mantel. Front and center was this one, from C. S. Lewis's *The Screwtape Letters*:

> The humans live in time but [God] destines them to eternity. He therefore, I believe, wants them to attend chiefly to two things, to eternity itself, and to that point of time which they call the Present. For the Present is the point at which time touches

eternity . . . He would therefore have them continually concerned either with eternity (which means being concerned with Him) or with the Present . . . obeying the present voice of conscience, bearing the present cross, receiving the present grace, giving thanks for the present pleasure.[15]

I don't know how many times, as a single thirty-something, I stood in front of the mantel reading those words. They felt like a telegram from God, calling me away from my dreams and fears about the future, and back to the present. I looked at them again during the months we waited for Toby, and I should be looking at them now, during this wait for an unknown baby, who may or may not ever make it into my arms.

Staying focused on the present moment is a constant struggle for you, Emily. It still can be a struggle for me, too, but by now, I know it's a problem and can fight against it. You don't. Not yet. Your mind is always running out ahead of you, making plans, dreaming dreams, looking forward to some imaginary life. And you don't even try to stop it. You give your mind and heart free rein to dwell in the future, in the someday when you think your season of waiting will end—when you're married, a mother, and doing work you love.

When you live that way, though, the season of waiting never ends. One season of waiting just gives way to another season of waiting, because there is always something for which you can wait. First, it's the husband. Then the baby. Then another baby. After that, you're waiting for the baby to sleep through the night, go to school, head off to college, and then have babies of their own. Every day you're alive, the future will stretch out before you, giving you something to anticipate, to think about, to focus on. And because it's an imaginary future, with no real sufferings or inconveniences in it, it will always be more attractive than the life you're living. This is why living for the future always breeds discontent with the present. A real imperfect present can never compare to an imagined perfect future.

But this imperfect present is all any of us are promised, Emily. The present is where God meets us. The present is where He calls us. The present is where He has work for us to do and people for us to love and grace for us to receive. The life you dream of in your head isn't your life. This is your life. Right now. Today. And while you look toward tomorrow, you're missing it.

This is another reason you're dropping the ball on living the feminine genius. You've become so focused on the future and what you don't have that you can't appreciate what you do have. You say you long to give yourself to a husband and children, but your thoughts are so consumed with that longing that you're not giving yourself to the people standing right in front of you—your roommates, your coworkers, your own family. These are the people to whom God has called you to give yourself today. You're also not taking advantage of all the opportunities God is giving you, for learning, growing, and healing, because they're not the opportunities you want. You're waiting for what you want, but missing what you need.

Stop waiting, Emily. Stop thinking about the next season in life, and make this season count. Lean into now. Work on growing in virtue now. Work on overcoming bad habits and besetting sins now. Grow closer to Jesus now. Spend time with Him now. Also, walk through the doors He's opening now. And last but not least, lavish love on the people God has put in your life now. Today, in this season of life, they are your vocation. They are your path to holiness.

No matter how old we are or what season of life we're in, these are the things God asks of us. How we answer Him in each season shapes the seasons to come. Every yes you give to God now allows Him to plant a seed in your life that will bear fruit later on.

I wouldn't be here, Emily, with my husband and baby, writing to you, if I hadn't eventually figured this out. Sometime in my late twenties, I stopped waiting for a husband to show up and started doing all the things I thought I had to wait until marriage to do. I bought a house. I renovated it. I quit my full-time job writing for the university and began freelancing from home. I wrote essays and books and Bible studies. I hosted dinner parties for families. I took friends' daughters to see the Nutcracker. I had slumber parties with my nieces, and I traveled to Europe every year.

All those things didn't just keep me busy until Chris and Toby came along. They led me to them. They readied me for them. They helped me grow in wisdom, patience, and love, so I could be a better wife and mother than I would have otherwise been. More important, they led me closer to God. They helped me grow in understanding of who He is and how He loves us. They made me more the woman He created me to be.

Remember, that's the goal. Not a wedding ring. Not one baby or two or three. Not a new house or a big house or a clean house. But everlasting life with Jesus Christ.

Don't wait until the next season arrives to pursue that goal. Waiting won't make the next season any better. It will do the opposite; it will make it worse. It will make it harder and less fruitful. And someday, you will run out of seasons. None of us is guaranteed a next one. None of us is guaranteed a tomorrow. So focus on now. Whenever your mind tries to run ahead of itself and borrow grace or trouble from the future, call it back. Ask God to show you the work of the moment and help you receive the grace of the moment. Because that's all we're offered.

Telling you this is a good reminder that when I get home from this trip, I need to stop focusing on an adoption that may never happen and attend to more immediate problems. Like the basement. Or the garage. Organizing is always a great way to call your mind back to the present. So are toddlers, and I hear one waking up. As always, praying for you.

Blessings,
Emily

23

"YOU DO BELONG."

July 7, 2020
Hawthorne House

Dear Emily,
We're home. We made the drive in record time: eleven hours, door to door. And that was with an almost two-year-old. I spent most of yesterday doing laundry, and that's the agenda for today as well. I did receive an email yesterday morning, though, that I wanted to share with you.

The woman who sent it is older, like me—in her late thirties or early forties, I'm guessing. She's also married, like me, and barren, like me, which is why she wrote. She wanted to thank me for writing about my struggle with infertility. She said it made her feel less alone. "I think the Church might have a place for me after all," she concluded.

I wrote back to her, thanking her for the kind words. I wanted to write more, but Toby needed chasing or feeding or saving, so I kept my response short. I'll tell you what I wanted to tell her, though, because this feeling of not belonging is a feeling you know well.

With your red hair and fairer-than-fair skin, you didn't look like anyone in your family or your class at school. You lost track of the times you were called Casper during recess or asked if you were adopted. You stopped wearing shorts so no one could joke about your legs blinding them. In grade school, you repeatedly faked illness to avoid the teasing. In high school, you retreated to the library. In Anne of Green Gables, Emily of New Moon, and Elizabeth Bennet, you found friends who understood you, who didn't tease you for using big words or having even bigger ideas. Your book friends were your most treasured companions until you left for college, where, finally, you found friends who loved you for who you were.

Life got easier after that. In some ways, it's stayed easier. You've never lacked for friends since. Partly because you grew into your vocabulary. Also, because red hair and fair skin aren't the liabilities in adulthood that they were on the Jordan Catholic School playground.

But soon, Emily, as all your friends marry off, you will feel alone again. And when their babies come fast and furious, you'll feel even more alone. Your friends will love you, their babies will love you, and you will always feel like you belong in their homes. In church on Sunday, though, when you sit alone, surrounded by pews filled to bursting with beautiful Catholic families, you will feel like the strange, awkward, redheaded child all over again, unseen, misunderstood, out of place in a world where you don't belong.

Here, however, is what you won't know: almost every other woman in church feels the same.

The other single women feel like they don't belong because they don't have a ring on their finger. The infertile women feel like they don't belong because they don't have a baby in their arms. The woman whose uterus was ravaged by cancer feels like she doesn't belong because she only has two children in her pew, while the woman with six children and another in her belly feels like she doesn't belong because her family is so much bigger than everyone else's. The working woman feels like she doesn't belong because she spends her days in an office. The black and brown women feel like they don't belong because they're worshipping in a sea of white faces. The single mom feels like she doesn't belong because she is on her own, in Mass and everywhere else. And the mom of the daughter with special needs feels like she doesn't belong because her little girl can't behave in Mass like the other little girls do.

I could go on. Every woman at some point kneels in a church . . . or works in an office . . . or walks into a party where she feels like she doesn't belong. Where she feels different. Where she thinks people see her as "other."

And some do. There's no denying that. Some Irish Catholics do see someone with beautiful dark skin worshipping in their parish and don't want her there. Some homeschooling moms do look at the working mom and judge her a failure. Some wealthy suburbanite women do cast withering glances at the homeschooling mom whose kids are dressed in thrift store threads.

But most women? They're not judging. They're too busy feeling judged. They don't have time to conclude that you don't belong at Mass on a Sunday morning because they're too occupied with their own fear of not belonging. I promise you, nobody thinks about you as much as you do.

One of the reasons God made us different from one another, giving us complementary strengths and experiences, was to show us that we're made for communion—with others and Him. Each of us is never enough because we weren't created to be enough. We were created to need one another so that we can be gifts to one another. All that's different about us should draw us together, with the woman with one child learning from the woman with six, the woman with no decorating skills benefitting from the friend with tons, and the mom with full hands getting a break from her friend with empty arms.

Those differences should also remind us that just as we need each other, we need God more. Only His truth can guide us. Only His love can heal us. Only His life can make us whole.

We miss those lessons when we turn in on ourselves, focusing on our own grievances or shortcomings to the exclusion of all else. When we do that, we become blind to how desperately lonely, hurting, or lost the other women around us feel. We also miss out on the gifts that the women who are nothing like us are meant to be to us.

Renounce the voice that says you don't belong, Emily. Then, reach out to the woman not like you. Include her. Affirm her. Learn from her. And let her learn from you. You do belong. In the Church. In the world. To each other.

Blessings,
Emily

24

"YOU ARE MORE THAN A NUMBER ON A SCALE."

July 9, 2020
Hawthorne House

Dear Emily,

Today, we need to talk about your weight. Not whatever number the scale read when you stood on it this morning. Rather, we need to talk about how you feel about that number . . . and how you will feel about that number as it inches up in the years to come.

I hesitate to do this, because your struggles with your weight and your appearance go so deep, and I don't have time today to give these struggles the attention they deserve. So many different issues have fed into your eating disorder, and most of them have nothing to do with food. Your desire for control, your struggle with cultural conceptions of femininity, your belief that you don't deserve to eat—all those struggles have played a role in your long, slow starvation.

Healing is coming, though. Healing is coming soon. Before your twenty-sixth birthday, God will do a great work in you and lead you out of the dark place in which you've hid for so long. You are going to learn to love food—both cooking it and eating it. You're going to learn to love your body, too. Well, maybe not love it. But you will learn to value it and care for it. And you will have no desire to do anything less.

You will definitely have days when you're not thrilled with how your body looks. Like . . . today. Between turning forty-five, all the hormone-altering fertility drugs I took before that, and the demands of working from home while raising a baby, I have put on more weight than I care to admit. I miss my pretty clothes that have been hanging in our attic closet for the past two years. I miss seeing myself in pictures and not flinching. I miss my old body.

I don't miss my old life though, and honestly, I'm not the least inclined to do anything about the weight anytime soon. There's no time. And really, there's no need. I eat well. I'm still reasonably fit. And nobody cares about my size but me. Not Chris. Not Toby. Not a single friend or family member. Not a single stranger I pass on the street.

This is what I want you to understand. After you've worked through all the other issues contributing to the eating disorder and come out on the other side, please know that nobody but you cares whether you are a size four, a size eight, or a size twelve. Nobody but you is interested in your weight. It is, literally, the least interesting thing about you.

When people look at you, they see a person, not a number. They see your smile, the glow of your skin, and the intelligence in your eyes. They see you, the woman and friend they love. And if you gain five pounds or ten pounds or twenty pounds? Guess what? They still see the woman and friend they love. They don't think about the weight. They think about how kind you are to them, how welcoming you are, and how attentive you are. They think about how happy, thoughtful, and intelligent you are. They appreciate it when you laugh at their jokes and ask them questions about their life. They love it when you affirm them and encourage them. They really love it when you feed them, too. That's what people will want from you, Emily: your love, your encouragement, your food. Not for you to look like a supermodel.

And Toby and Chris? The very things you hate about your body are the things they will love. Your curves and softness will be beautiful to both of them. You're their home. You're a warm, cozy place where they always can find comfort and love.

By the time you are me, you're not going to look like a girl anymore. You will look like a mother, an old mother. Or maybe a "mature mother" sounds nicer. Regardless, this look is a good thing! It's how you're supposed to look. It's who you are. The body expresses the person, remember? And your body at forty-five will say to the world that you are a woman who loves, who is fruitful even though she's never borne a baby, who is tender and safe, warm and generous. Your eyes will say that. Your smile will say that. Your curves will say that.

I know I keep talking about the devil. I honestly don't think much about him . . . until I sit down to write you. But, when I look at how so many women—you included—hate their feminine curves and long for bodies that are more angular and masculine, I can't help but feel that he is behind it. It's like Satan doesn't only want to stop women from exercising our feminine genius; he also wants to destroy the physical manifestation of it. He wants us to hate the very look of motherhood and associate beauty only with prepubescent barrenness.

More fundamentally, though, Satan wants to distract us. He wants us to waste our time, energy, and emotions on something as insignificant as a number on a scale.

Your struggle with your eating disorder is not insignificant, Emily. You are hurting, and you need healing. But when I, me, today waste time fretting about my weight? When my forty-five-year-old self doesn't want to be in pictures with Toby because I think I'm too heavy? I am being ridiculous.

I have a toddler who depends on me every second he is awake. I have friends who need my attention, a husband who needs my love, and a God who keeps giving me more writing to do than I can handle. I also have dishes to wash, a basement to organize, and prayers to offer. Every second I spend fretting about how my stomach isn't perfectly flat anymore is a second I am not doing what God needs me to do.

Eating healthy is important. Exercise is good. The body was made to be nourished by good food and kept strong by movement. But the body was made *for* love. It was made *for* communion. It was made *for* prayer, work, friendship, hugging, kissing, laughing, cooking, and dancing with your toddler at five o'clock in the afternoon. You need to be healthy to do those things. But healthy is so much more than the number you would prefer to see on a scale. You are so much more than the number you would prefer to see on the scale.

Let the number go, Emily. As the years go by and your eating disorder becomes a thing of the past, don't eat too much, but don't eat too little either. Enjoy your cheesecake. Enjoy your carbs. Don't worry, when your baby is small, that you can't exercise as much and as often as you did before he came. Your body will be so much more lovely at forty-five than it is at twenty-five. All the sufferings you've endured, all the work you've done, all the friends you've served, the diapers you've changed, meals you've cooked, tears you've wiped, hands you've held, hearts you've encouraged, apologies you've made—all that love will write itself on your body, making it beautiful.

Give thanks for that. Praise Jesus for that. And when the devil suggests you waste one precious minute of your life lamenting your beautiful, beloved body or worrying about a number on the scale, go ahead and tell him where he can go. God's got a lot of work for you to do, and you don't have time to entertain the devil's nonsense.

Blessings,
Emily

On Social Media

·ᴖᴖᴖ·
25

"VIRTUAL LIFE IS NOT REAL LIFE."

July 13, 2020
Hawthorne House

Dear Emily,

It's time to talk about social media. I have precious few practical skills to teach you for the end times. I can't start a fire without matches. I don't know how to shoot a gun or skin a rabbit. I am useless at a campsite. If a zombie apocalypse is imminent, I'm a goner. But what I can do is help you navigate social media with a modicum of wisdom. And for this stage of the apocalypse, that may be the most important skill you need.

So, social media. Even after all these letters, it's still a meaningless term to you, isn't it? How did I describe it in my first letter? As an AOL chat room, only with pretty pictures (occasionally) and a billion unmannered, opinionated people (always)? That's probably about right.

The various forms of social media are online platforms—some for posting news, others for posting pictures, all for posting opinions. On those platforms, hundreds of millions of people spend an inordinate amount of time, some sharing their life with friends and family, more arguing with strangers. Occasionally, people keep their online world small, limiting it to people they know in real life. Most people don't limit it that strictly, however, and find themselves part of an online world that is bigger than anyone's world was meant to be. This includes me.

For you, in 2020, this world will consist of three forms of social media. More forms exist, and your teenage niece uses some of them, but for now you only need to worry about Twitter, Facebook, and Instagram.

With few exceptions, Twitter is a dumpster fire of hot air and ego. You have to lurk there a little for professional reasons, but it's generally best avoided. The temptation to despair of humanity is strong these days. You don't need further temptation.

Facebook is manageable if you follow the right people (those who post interesting articles) and unfollow the wrong ones (those prone to constant arguing). It's also important to know which topics to avoid (politics, masks, pandemics, vaccines, immigration, race, abortion, homosexuality, transgenderism, the liturgy, and maybe a few hundred more), as well as which things to post (baby pictures . . . just not pictures of babies in car seats).

Instagram used to be lovely—Facebook's gentle, kind, understanding little sister, who knew how to let people be wrong and brought women together to focus on our common love for pretty houses, cute babies, and good food. Unfortunately, it's now going through something of an identity crisis and is no longer quite so gentle or understanding. 2020 has done that to us all.

I'm being rough on social media, though. For an extrovert like me, who works out of her home, it can be a Godsend. I've met wonderful people online who have become real-life friends. It can serve as a powerful tool for evangelization. And without it, we wouldn't have Toby or be in a place to adopt another baby. Friends, followers, and perfect strangers have helped us with every aspect of our adoptions, from finding ethical adoption professionals to fundraising. Whenever I'm tempted to despair of social media, I look at Toby, and I'm reminded of the profound generosity of men and women who have loved our family without even knowing us.

So, it's not all bad. There can be great goodness on the Interwebs. If you want to experience that goodness, though, you have to be good. You have to use social media well.

I have quite a few thoughts on what this means, but today, let's start with this: virtual life is not real life. It's one dimensional. It doesn't allow you to see the whole of a person or the whole of a life.

With some people, social media only allows you to see a carefully crafted and curated image. Not their struggles. Not their sorrows. Not their messes. No matter how many pretty pictures someone might post, you don't know what's happening inside the four walls of their home or in the quiet recesses of their hearts. You don't know all the thoughts they're thinking, the conversations they're having, and the work they're doing (or not doing).

With others, it only shows you someone's brokenness. A person's fears, anger, or wounds leap off the screen as they rage and rant. But you don't know why they're raging and ranting. You don't know what happened to them this morning, let alone five, ten, or fifty years ago. You also only see the raging and ranting. Not their love for their grandchildren or their kindness to the homeless guy downtown or their humble confessions to a priest every Saturday, when they're wracked with guilt for losing their temper yet again.

The fullness of a person's virtue or vice can never be comprehended through a screen. Nor can it be measured by how they interact with others through those screens.

Someday, God will hold you accountable for how you used social media, Emily. You will have to answer for how you treated others, engaged others, and helped or hurt others online. But it's not the only thing for which He'll hold you accountable. God doesn't view us through a screen. He doesn't see only what we choose for Him to see. He sees all. So, He will judge all—the person we were online and the person we were offline.

You, however, don't see all. Which means you need to refrain from judging what only God can. Assume that everyone you interact with online is struggling. Assume they're both a little better and a little worse than they seem on social media. Then, try not to think too much about it.

Instead, think about the world your body inhabits— the three-dimensional one. Where people need you to look them in the eye and feed them, hug them, and serve them. Where conversations aren't limited to 280 or 2200 characters. Where the real work of talking through differences, healing from wounds, and growing in wisdom happens.

That's the world for which God made you. That's the world for which He took on a body. And that's the world He saved with His body. Jesus didn't Tweet the Good News. He didn't share the Gospel with a meme. He didn't atone for the world's sin with a status update. Instead, He chose to enter time in an age where none of those tools existed. Then, He proclaimed the Good News in the flesh, person to person, body to body. He lived the Gospel in the flesh, healing people with His hands, spittle, mud, and water. He atoned for sin in the flesh, offering His holy body for us. And He rose to new life in the flesh, so that we too could have life.

You can choose to be on social media or not, Emily. It's not a requirement of the Gospel that you have an Instagram account. But it is a requirement of the Gospel that you use your body to worship God and love your neighbor. Prioritize that. The more you do those things well, the easier navigating social media will become.

Blessings,
Emily

26

"BE DISCERNING."

July 14, 2020
Hawthorne House

Dear Emily,

People are angry with me. People who used to respect me no longer do. Not a lot of people, and most are strangers, but it stings.

You know this feeling. You may only be twenty-five, but the opinions that burst unthinkingly out of your mouth have ticked plenty of people off in those twenty-five years. Here's the irony, though: The people angry with me now are angry because I *won't* share my opinions. A couple years back, I set a strict rule for myself: no talking about current events online. So, no political opinions, no hot takes on news about the Church, no quick reactions to headlines about presidential politics. And some people don't like that with the real world falling apart, I'm not saying much about that in the virtual world.

My rule sounds incomprehensible to you, doesn't it? Having an audience of thousands of people, and not taking every opportunity to share my thoughts with them on the news of the day? Why on earth would I do that? That's your dream, and I'm thumbing my nose at it.

I promise, I don't have fewer opinions than I used to. If anything, I have more. Experience, however, has taught me to exercise more control over how and when to express those opinions. I know now, like you don't, that at certain times and in certain contexts, regardless of what other people want me to do, it's wrong to share my opinions. It's not helpful to others, and it's spiritually dangerous for me. That's particularly true when it comes to talking about the news of the day on social media.

Over the past twenty years, the Internet has gotten a heck of a lot louder than the Internet you know. It's not just writers reacting to news and sharing their opinions. It's everybody. Or almost everybody. It doesn't matter if your normal content is about paint colors or cookies, when something big happens in the world, everyone has an opinion. Everyone shares their opinion. Everyone demands everyone else's opinion. And they demand it right away.

For a while, I happily went along with those demands. For a time, I offered quick and copious commentary on what was happening in Washington, Rome, and wherever news broke. My reactions were instant, witty, and cutting. I got attention for that, and my audience grew.

Then, I started to realize a few things.

First, I realized that my instant commentary was often wrong. Sometimes, it was wrong because the news story to which I was reacting was wrong. Reporter bias influenced the story or there just wasn't enough information to ensure accurate reporting. Often, though, my commentary was wrong because I was wrong. I didn't know what I didn't know. So, I started to slow down, to pause for a few days or even weeks before posting reactions. As I did, I discovered that by not reacting immediately—by waiting, watching, and reading what people more knowledgeable than I had to say—the opinions I formed about events became more nuanced and thoughtful. They became more grounded in truth. Which is important.

Second, I realized that my online discussions about contentious topics weren't all that fruitful. More often, they were the opposite. They were destructive. They tempted me to write things I would never say to a person's face, and they tempted the people writing to me to do the same. Because I didn't know the person with whom I was engaging, because I couldn't see a face, hear a voice, and observe the one hundred different ways a body communicates, I said the wrong things, things that weren't helpful. And because people didn't know me, see me, or hear me, they interpreted my words through the lens of their own experience or wounds, often missing my point entirely. Eventually, I concluded that if I want my conversations about difficult topics to bear fruit, ninety-nine times out of one hundred, it's better for me to have those conversations in person, not online.

The third reason I stopped talking about politics and (most) current events online is because I didn't like how it affected me. I didn't like the person I was becoming. Fighting with strangers online hardened me. It cemented my opinions of my own rightness and righteousness. It prevented me from listening to others' stories and others' opinions. It tempted me to treat people who disagreed with me as less than human. It also tempted me to be more cutting, more sharp, more inflammatory. Because again, that's what got the likes. That's what got the follows. That's what got people sharing and resharing and telling me how brave I was, how good I was, and how I shouldn't listen to anyone who disagrees with me because they're part of the problem.

Last but not least, I started holding my tongue because I wasn't the only one being cutting online. Not by a long shot. Posts that reduced those on the other side of an issue to the evil "other" filled my feeds. From both left and right, I saw the same problems: an inability to love our enemies, a lack of respect for human freedom, and the absence of justice in the quest for justice. People who claimed to be Catholic, who claimed to be pro-life or anti-racist or a friend of the poor, refused to be friends with anyone who approached an issue even slightly differently from them. They misunderstood each other and misrepresented each other. They demonized the other. And not surprisingly, they didn't listen to one another. They still don't.

As a culture, we've forgotten we are brothers and sisters, made in the image of God. From that forgetting flows not only online vitriol but also every other injustice about which we're fighting.

So, that's what I decided to focus on. For the most part, I left writing about specific injustices behind and began focusing on helping people understand the love God has for them and the dignity of the human person. I hoped that if more people could experience that love and see that dignity, then they could finally start caring about justice.

I don't know if it's working. People are still yelling. But it is helping me. Listening while everyone else is talking is teaching me humility. It's also helping me grow in patience and compassion. I don't go on social media to be right anymore. I go on to listen and share what I think God wants me to share. Which makes for a more peaceful, loving Emily all around.

This way of engaging online isn't for everyone. Nor should it be. God has uniquely equipped and called some people to tackle the tough issues on social media. You're just not one of those people. It's bad for your soul. It's bad for a lot of people's souls. They would see this, if they took more time to reflect and discern.

Be discerning, Emily. Be discerning about what you post on social media. Be discerning about how it affects you. And be discerning about how it affects others. In an ongoing way, pause and ask yourself what fruit your online interactions are bearing and how those interactions are shaping your soul. Does what you post contribute to thoughtful discussions, or does it lead to polarizing arguments? Do your posts primarily attract people who are kind and respectful to your comment boxes, or do they attract people who are angry, bitter, and cruel?

And what about you? Are you becoming more thoughtful, more faithful, and more loving, both to those who agree with you and to those who disagree with you? Or are you becoming more angry, more hostile, more prone to rash judgement? Do your disagreements become personal? Can you disagree with someone without insulting them? Are you able to bear the wrongs done against you patiently? Is social media making it more difficult for you to see and treat everyone as the image of God? Is it exacerbating other sins with which you struggle—vanity, envy, greed, pride?

You also need to consider whether your posts and online interactions are becoming a source of scandal or an occasion of sin for others. Are you inviting people to belittle or dehumanize others? Are you allowing detraction or calumny in your comment sections? Are you fanning the flames of anger, hatred, or ignorance with polemical posts rooted in emotion rather than reason, facts, and faith? What is your writing or your sharing doing to other people's souls?

For some, this process of discernment will help them engage more fruitfully online. For others, it might make them do what I did and bow out of certain discussions or approach important topics from a different angle. Either way, it's this kind of discernment that will make us the kind of witnesses Pope Benedict XVI called for, the kind who enables "the infinite richness of the Gospel to find forms of expression capable of reaching the minds and hearts of all."[16]

You have to be your own harshest critic with social media, Emily. Online, it's easy to lock yourself in an echo chamber where you only hear the voices that offer agreement and praise. In that echo chamber, you can get comfortable. You can start to believe yourself righteous when you're anything but. Honest, ongoing discernment will help check that tendency. And you need to check it. No matter how right your opinions or how righteous your intentions, if what you post on social media is becoming an occasion of sin, for you or others, it's time to step back and reevaluate. You can't help Jesus win souls if you're destroying your own.

Blessings,
Emily

27

"BEWARE THE ONLINE MOB."

July 15, 2020
Hawthorne House

Dear Emily,

I saw a woman's life destroyed last week. A mob of people who called themselves Christians took her down. And they thought their work righteous.

The drama began when the woman made a questionable decision—one I wouldn't have made—and people criticized her for it. Not in person, but online, on a social media platform. She didn't explain her decision well, and so more people criticized her. They began posting about the controversy on their social media accounts, and that led to their friends and followers chiming in. As they did, the discussion (if you can call it that), ranged far beyond the original poor decision.

Some, without offering evidence, alleged that the woman (a graphic designer) had plagiarized their work. Others complained about the woman's online presence and the language she used to talk about her past. Rumors were repeated, insults lobbed, aspersions on character cast.

By the end of the week, the woman had lost many of her clients, her means of supporting her family, and her reputation. She had been quite effectively cancelled. And the online mob moved on to its next target, satisfied with its own righteousness, calling its work "holy."

Beware the online mob, Emily. Don't join in. Don't participate—no matter how righteous you think their cause might be and no matter how many people tell you the "call-out culture" is the work of the Lord, a participation in what Jesus did in the temple with a whip of His own, or akin to what the Old Testament prophets did for a wayward Israel.

As I have told you before, you are not Jesus. You have neither His perfect knowledge nor His perfect heart. Neither, please note, did Peter, James, or John. Which is probably why, when Jesus went into call-out mode, He always did it on His own. He didn't invite others to join in. He didn't sanction an unruly crowd raiding the temple along with Him.

The same goes for the prophets. Those men were singular individuals anointed by God to call Israel and its leaders back to holiness. They were given knowledge, words, and power from on high to carry out the work entrusted to them. And they engaged in that work with humility, knowing their soul was on the line if they judged rashly, spoke unfairly, or used their prophetic office to pursue personal vengeance. That's why nobody wanted to be a prophet. Jonah ran away. Moses tried to beg off and foist the job on his brother. Gideon and Jeremiah both told God He should find someone else. They all knew it was a thankless job that came with terrifying responsibility.

It still does. So don't confuse an online mob with Jesus or His prophets. Mobs are never holy. They are dangerous.

Whether their weapons are words or pitchforks, mobs perpetuate injustice in the quest for justice. The initial outrage may be justified. A wrong may need righting. But mobs get out of control. They give cover to other evils, allowing people with hurting or darkened hearts to act out on their baser emotions, with less fear of reprisal. They present to countless souls a near occasion for sin, which then becomes, for many, an actual occasion for sin.

In person, the sin is often the wanton destruction of life and property. Online, it's the wanton destruction of a person's reputation. It's easy to minimize the latter form of destruction, but the Church warns against this, explaining that to damage the reputation of another is to sin against the eighth commandment, which calls us to always bear witness to the truth. The *Catechism* explains:

> *Respect for the reputation* of persons forbids every attitude and word likely to cause them unjust injury. He becomes guilty:
> - of *rash judgment* who, even tacitly, assumes as true, without sufficient foundation, the moral fault of a neighbor;
> - of *detraction* who, without objectively valid reason, discloses another's faults and failings to persons who did not know them;
> - of *calumny* who, by remarks contrary to the truth, harms the reputation of others and gives occasion for false judgments concerning them. (2477)

Online mobs don't just damage reputations, though. They damage the Church. They give scandal to Catholics and non-Catholics alike, who see the lack of Christian charity in discussions where name calling, insults, and gossip abound, and wonder at how people who claim to follow Christ can treat each other so cruelly. When we tear each other apart in public, with no mercy and no love, we aren't witnesses to the Faith; we are witnesses against the Faith. We commit the sin of scandal.

I hear the redhead in you protesting: But what if you know the fault in the other is real? What if they really did do something wrong? What if *not* publicly standing against them leads to scandal?

Those are good questions, and you need to think through them carefully in particular situations. As you do, ask yourself a few more questions.

Have you verified all the facts, or are you reacting to another's version of events?

Are you giving the person the benefit of the doubt and construing their words or actions in the most charitable light?

Do you know for certain the person's intent was sinful, or are you unfairly judging another's heart and motivations?

Must you disclose the sin publicly, or can you pursue justice by another means?

Is it possible to critique the person's ideas or actions without going after the person?

Is there a way to deal with the problem privately, either by talking to the person directly or by talking to someone who knows the person—who has authority over them or who can respond more directly to the problem?

In attacking the person publicly, are you giving the problem undeserved attention—attention that will inflate the person's sense of importance or harden them in their sin?

Is it good for your soul to go after the person publicly? Does it fill you with pride or vanity? Does it tempt you to rash judgement or detraction? Does it feel good to be called righteous by the other members of the mob? Are your motives truly disinterested, or do you personally stand to gain something by calling out this person?

Is your wading into the fray or even leading the charge against another person creating a near occasion of sin for another?

Do you yourself particularly need to publicly protest this action? Does your voice add something important or necessary?

Above all, are you acting out of love and with love, showing kindness and respect for the person as you correct them?

The time may come when you do need to publicly criticize or disassociate yourself from someone. But before you do, go over the questions above and be honest with yourself. And if you are in danger of leading a mob or getting sucked into a mob, run as fast as you can in the opposite direction. You don't want to feed the call-out culture or cancel culture. Not just because each of us will be held accountable for every life we offered up to that beast. But also, because one day, the beast you feed will feed on you.

Blessings,
Emily

28

"LET PEOPLE BE WRONG."

July 16, 2020
Hawthorne House

Dear Emily,

It's been a rough week on the adoption front. Cases are coming in fast and furious again, but so are the nos. We've had three this week already. One was particularly hard: a baby boy, whose mom reminded me of Toby's birth mom. I wanted her to choose us so badly. Given what we went through in the months leading up to Toby's birth, I felt especially equipped to love this mom and handle the struggles the baby might have. She felt otherwise. So, I'm going to organize the basement instead of getting ready for a new baby.

Before I head downstairs, though, I want to talk with you about the secret to finding peace on social media (and in life to some extent). It's simple, but effective. Not easy. But simple. The secret is this: Let people be wrong.

Really. Let them. It is not your job to correct every stranger on the Internet. It is not up to you to ensure that every person who follows you or whom you follow has the exact right opinion about immigration or baby sleep training or how to cook risotto. People are allowed to like Taylor Swift, no matter how misguided you think that is. If someone intends to become a vegan or vote for a politician

159

whom you think is dumber than a box of rocks, you don't have to jump into their comment boxes and tell them all the reasons you disagree with their intentions.

If someone on Twitter is arguing back and forth with your cousin about abortion, you don't have to jump into the fray. You can let them continue their discussion and keep scrolling.

If a person you follow on Instagram is passionate about environmental stewardship and you think all their posting about it is frivolous given the other problems in the world, you don't have to tell them that. Let them talk about what they care about, and then, in your posts, talk all the more about what you care about.

And if someone takes you to task in direct messages for pursuing a second adoption or not speaking up about the election or seeing family in the middle of the pandemic, you can thank them kindly for their opinion and leave it at that. You don't have to argue with them. You don't have to defend yourself. You don't have to convince them why you're right and they're wrong. You can just let them be wrong.

You can do this because some things really are a matter of opinion. Some people like beets, running, and sleeping outside in the cold under a tent. There is nothing objectively good or bad about lots of things in life, and your preferences don't have to be everyone's.

Some things are also a matter of calling. Environmental stewardship is important. So is stopping human trafficking, standing up for the unborn, opposing racism, and ending the persecution of the marginalized, not to mention helping people think clearly about metaphysics,

Christology, and liturgy. We have an abundance of pressing problems in this world, and different people will feel called to focus their time and energy on different issues. They get to make that call. It's not about you. It's not up to you. You have your work to do. They have theirs. And every second you waste getting mad at someone for doing the work they're called to do is a second you're not doing the work you're called to do.

You also can let people be wrong on weightier matters—on things that are objectively right and wrong—because frankly, arguing with strangers online is one of the most fruitless tasks known to man. In the history of the world, the number of people who have walked away from a Twitter argument with their mind changed is exactly three. Maybe four. Most people shut down or double down when they're berated by strangers. Especially in public. It's human nature. Which is why in-person conversations, between people who have a real relationship (and without an audience), tend to bear so much more fruit than online arguments.

Even more fundamentally, you can let people be wrong because that's what God does. He gives us the freedom to be wrong.

God does not force His will on anyone. He gives us the moral law. He gives us practical guidance about how to follow that law, plus the grace to follow it well. He also lets us know there will be natural consequences to not following the moral law. But He doesn't make us follow it. He doesn't compel us to love Him, believe in Him, or obey Him. He lets us make choices that He would rather us not make. And we do. We do it all the time. But God keeps on loving us anyway.

Occasionally, I find myself wondering why God gave us free will. It often seems like the world would be a much better place if He would take it away, leaving us with no choice but to do the right thing. There would be so much less suffering. But then, I remember that there would also be so much less love. Because love, to be love, has to be freely given. You can't bully a person into love.

From all eternity, God saw how much suffering free will would bring into the world. He also saw how much love it would bring. And, in the balance, He judged the love worth it. So, if God thinks giving people the freedom to be wrong is worth the cost, who am I to question?

And yes, there will be times where you need to engage with someone's different opinion or defend yourself. When you think it's important, you can jump into the fray and say your piece or make your case or share whatever knowledge you have. Pray first, though, before you argue or correct.

As you pray, ask yourself why you feel the need to engage. Do you have some unique knowledge or understanding that could deepen the conversation? Do you have a relationship or history of engagement that gives you some hope the person in question might listen to you? Can you engage them, thoughtfully, with a spirit of love and mercy? Do you have to do it publicly, or can you take the conversation out of the comment boxes or offline? Do you want this person's best? Or do you just want to prove yourself right? Lastly, ask yourself, Is this the best use of your time at this present moment? Is this what God wants you to do, or is there other, more pressing, more important work that you are neglecting?

If the answer to any of those questions is no, then move right along. Keep scrolling. Or better yet, log off and build a tower with your baby.

Again, this isn't easy. Letting people be wrong is hard. Letting people be wrong about being wrong is even harder. Because many people won't show you the same respect you show them. They won't assume the best about you. They will want to argue. They will want to insult you. They will want to shame you. But again, you can't control them. You can't force anyone to engage how you want to engage. So pray. Be open to correction. Search your heart every day. And when you fail, which you will, apologize and offer it up to God. He understands. He loves you. Even when you're wrong.

On that note, I have a basement to organize.

Blessings,
Emily

29

"BE YOU."

July 17, 2020
Hawthorne House

Dear Emily,

I've said a lot about what not to do on social media, haven't I? Don't become a near occasion for sin. Don't join an online mob. Don't get into pointless arguments with strangers. There's more you shouldn't do—like, don't talk about Harry Potter, don't tell anyone when you go on vacation in 2020, and don't take that "What Disney Princess Are You?" quiz. It's a phishing scheme run by Russian hackers.

I think I need to stop with the don'ts, however, and focus on the dos. Here's the first one: Do be you.

God has done something in your life, Emily, that He has done in no other. Your story is singular. So is every other person's story. Every one of us has a unique tale to tell of sin and grace, sorrow and joy, hope and fulfillment. We each carry a part of the salvation story in our heart—some working out of what happened on the cross and in the tomb. The world needs to see those stories. Share yours.

Let people see how God has moved in your life. Let them hear the wisdom He's entrusted to you. Let them watch you struggle with hope and suffer with trust and flounder with faith. Show them beauty where you find it—in an organized pantry, a freshly painted room, the face of a sleeping baby. But don't be afraid to let them see the messes, too. Those are also beautiful.

God is a God of order, but two thousand years ago He became Man and entered into the chaos of the world. Through His Spirit, in the Church, He abides here still. He's in the crazy, the messy, and the wild of your life as much as He's in the calm, the lovely, and the curated. More maybe, because it's in the crazy that we remember our need for Him the most. Letting people see your messes is letting people see your need for God. That helps them remember they need Him, too.

It's okay if you want to use filters for the pictures you post. When you've spent the night with a thirty-two-pound toddler sleeping on top of you, you will need all the help you can get. But don't put a filter on your soul or your life. Don't try to be someone you're not. Don't pretend for the Internet. Share your life and your story as you experience it.

You don't have to spill your dirty laundry to fifteen thousand people (I advise against this). You don't have to weep online when you're having a bad day (call your best friends instead). But you do have to be you—writing in the same voice with which you speak, sharing what's on your heart, not trying to say what you think people want to hear or what will get you the most follows or shares. Just say the things you'd say to a friend over coffee. You can joke (a lot). You can complain (a little). You can rant (occasionally). Just bring yourself—your whole, beautiful, imperfect self to social media. That will be a gift.

That's the first "do." The second is this: Be a witness.

When you go online—to Instagram or Facebook (or

Twitter if you must), you can share interesting essays, articles, and posts. You can share baby pictures, home pictures, and food pictures. You can share what you're interested in, doing, and trying. But whatever you choose to share, never forget that the most important thing you have to share, online and in the world, is the Faith. It's Jesus Christ, alive in His Church. And the way you most effectively share the Faith online isn't by writing about it, but by embodying it.

As a Christian, as a Catholic, you are a witness to Christ. Accordingly, your every interaction online—with the news, with the culture, with people—should reflect Him. It should reflect His mercy, His goodness, His truth, His beauty, His compassion, and His deep and abiding care for every single human person.

You're not going to be a perfect witness to Christ—online or off. But do what you can to show kindness and respect to all those with whom you interact. Appreciate the people who come to your corner of the Internet to hear what you have to say. Don't belittle people or insult people. Treat everyone as an individual, with a face, a story, and a soul. Don't lump them into ideological categories or political groups. See the person, not the politics. Listen to their story. Assume the best always. Be kind, even when they're not kind to you. Pray for those who hurt you. Forgive them, too. Remember, there are a great many bruised reeds and smoldering wicks in this world, so be gentle as you proclaim the truth. Lead with compassion. End with mercy. Above all, remember that unlike Jesus, you are a sinner. Your judgements will not be perfect. Neither will your words. Be slow to form both. And quick to take back the ones that are wrong.

One last do: Do find common ground. Help others find it, too.

The way of the world is to divide us, segregate us, and isolate us, making us forget we are all one people, sharing one human nature. Social media can be a tool the devil uses to further divide us, or it can be a tool the Holy Spirit uses to reunite us. Seek to use it as a tool of the Holy Spirit.

When the world is falling apart, it's tempting to think that showing pictures of cute babies, organized mudrooms, and pretty dresses is a waste of time, that we should be doing the far more important work of arguing about politics or sharing news about injustice. But more often than you can imagine, the most important thing we can share on social media is video of a baby laughing or a father dancing with his little girl. Now, more than ever, we need points of connection. We need signposts of our shared humanity. We need reminders that we are brothers and sisters who all want to love and be loved, who dance with our children and weep with exhaustion and rejoice over a good meal or a freshly made bed or fat baby cheeks.

Those little, mundane, seemingly inconsequential things are actually of inestimable importance. They're the moments that make up a life, moments where grace quietly works in our hearts, transforming us, making us new. We all have them. We all live them. They connect us, binding us together across cultural and ideological divides. They humanize the Internet, depoliticizing it, bringing us back to the simple truth of who we are: men and women made in the image of God.

We are more alike than we are different. And helping people see that can help us engage each other's opinions more deeply, more charitably, and more fruitfully.

Okay, time to head back to the basement. Maybe I should show that mess to the Internet. That would be keeping it real!

Blessing,
Emily

On New Motherhood

·⌒◎⌒·
30

"MOTHERHOOD IS BORN OF SUFFERING."

July 25, 2020
The Schwartz Home

Dear Emily,

We have a son, a new one, a baby boy. The call came five days ago, at 4:24 p.m., on Monday afternoon. Chris and I were on the porch swing. Toby was playing nearby. The phone rang, and I saw it was Kim, our adoption consultant. We were surprised. We weren't waiting to hear back about any new cases. There were no moms that we knew of looking at our profile. We wondered what she could want. I answered.

"A baby boy was born yesterday in Dallas," she began. "He's your son if you want him. How soon could you get there?"

We pulled out of the driveway two hours later. Twenty-eight hours after that, we pulled into our friends' driveway. We would have gone straight to the hospital, but stupid bureaucratic restrictions meant we couldn't see him. As soon as the sun rose Wednesday morning, though, we were there, signing the papers. After that, we met our son. We named him Becket.

I wasn't planning on writing any letters to you about motherhood. As of today, I've been a mom for exactly two years. I'm still learning the shape and feel of it. I've never even potty trained a child. The advice I have to give is limited. But since I don't think I'm going to be able to think of much else besides motherhood for now, over the next couple of weeks I'll try share those thoughts with you. No advice on raising teenagers. Only what I've experienced. Only thoughts on these first, early, crazy, blessed years.

That being said, I'm not sure how much time I'll actually have to write while we're here, or even how long we'll be in Dallas. We found out when we got to the hospital on Wednesday that Becket was born much earlier than they first realized. He is precious, beautiful, holy, and perfect in every way that matters. He is just going to need more time in the NICU.

Fortunately, there are no major issues. Once he starts eating and gaining weight, we can go home. He won't eat, though. The little man will take a few milliliters of milk and then give up. I believe he could eat if he wanted to, but I'm not sure he wants to. Maybe he's thinking about his first mom—missing her voice and smell and heartbeat. Maybe he thinks he's not supposed to be here if she's not. Maybe he doesn't know what to do without her.

I don't know what his little mind knows or remembers. I might be imposing my own thoughts on his. Because I *am* thinking about his first mom, almost every minute of every day. With Toby, we spent seven months forming a relationship with his birthparents and knew without a doubt that adoption was the best possible choice for both Toby and them.

Not with Becket's first mom. We've never met her. Never talked to her. And while the adoption agency keeps telling us that his mom feels confident adoption is the best choice for her, and that we're the best family for him, I wish I could hear that from her. I want her to say those words to me, and I want to see the look in her eyes while she says them.

Because that hasn't happened, I sit here, all day, holding the baby she carried in her womb for thirty-four weeks, and I think about her. I think about how she feels now and about how she'll feel ten years from now. I fear she is adding grief to grief and trauma to trauma. I worry she will regret this. I worry she will grow bitter and hard without her baby in her life. And I worry she will show up in a week or a month or a year and ask to have Becket back.

I desperately want to talk to her. I want to reassure her that she doesn't have to do this if she doesn't want to. I want her to know that I want what's best for her and her baby, and if it's not us, I don't want that. But she doesn't want to talk to me. So, I sit here worrying. That's making it almost impossible for me to think of this baby in my arms as mine. I still think of him as hers. I'm scared to love him as my own.

I know this feeling will pass. As more weeks go by, he will become mine. But this fear of attaching is a whole new motherhood-shaped cross that I hadn't anticipated.

I should have anticipated it, though. This is the curse of Eve. "I will greatly multiply your pain in childbearing; in pain you shall bring forth children" (Gen 3:16).

You know this verse. You've read it a hundred times. Only, you think God is being literal, talking about contractions, pushing, and episiotomies. But God is never just literal, Emily. He means what He says. And He means more. This is what the Church calls the two "senses" of Scripture: literal and spiritual. The words on the page are the literal sense; they're true as written. The spiritual sense flows from the literal sense; it doesn't contradict the literal meaning, but deepens it, shedding new light on how that particular Scripture passage applies to the life of faith, the moral life, or life in the world to come. Which is why the curse of Eve can be about so much more than physical pain. It also can be about more than physical motherhood. For motherhood in all its forms—physical, adoptive, foster, spiritual—is born of suffering.

For some, that suffering looks like months of nausea, back pain, and bed rest . . . or ovarian wedge resections, letrozole, and progesterone shots. For others, it looks like home studies, humiliating fundraisers, and months of rejection. It can look like depression and anxiety, before and after birth. It can look like worry—about finances, birth defects, or how on earth you will handle another baby when you're barely surviving with the ones you have. It also can look like rejection from your family, the father's family, or even the father. It can look like realizing you've chained yourself forever to a man who is all wrong for you. It can mean enduring the scorn or pity of others. It can mean navigating the frustrating complexities of courts and caseworkers and birth parents consumed by their own struggles. It can mean letting a dream die, so a baby can live.

For other women, the suffering can look like letting go of your desire for physical children altogether and accepting the call to spiritual motherhood—of doing all the dying to self required to make space in your heart or home or life for someone who needs you. And, as I'm realizing today, it can look like trying to make room in your heart for a baby when fear and sorrow for another's grief are trying to crowd that baby out.

It's all a kind of death. None of us gets to do the life-giving work of mothering without some kind of dying.

That death, though, is followed by resurrection. It's followed by new life—the new life of the child and (or) your new life as mother. The blessing is eternally greater than the curse, Emily. Motherhood is worth the pain. It's worth the waiting. It's worth the worry and the work and the change it demands. I know this. Every day with Toby has taught me this. So, if it's worth all that, it must also be worth overcoming the fear of attaching to a baby whom you are terrified you will lose because he never belonged to you in the first place.

Wherever Becket's first mom is, I hope she knows I will always honor her motherhood. She died twice over, both in bringing her baby into the world and then letting him go because she believed it was best for him. She is a true mother. I pray I can be as good of a mother to Becket as she was.

Blessings,
Emily

"HOLD ON TO THOSE BABIES."

August 3, 2020
The Schwartz Home

Dear Emily,
Another day, another pre-NICU visit missive.

I've been heading up there every morning around eight and leaving at five, when Chris arrives. The days are long, away from Toby. The nights are long, away from Becket. I'm not sure where I'm supposed to be, because no matter where I am, I feel like I'm neglecting someone or failing someone. Welcome to being the mother of two, I guess.

It's good, though—this time with Becket. We just sit there, he and I, for nine hours at a stretch, skin to skin, heart to heart. I leave once during those nine hours, to eat and use the restroom. Other than that, I don't leave. I don't move.

The nurses think I'm crazy. I'm okay with that. I know this time is fleeting, and that once I'm home, with Toby and Chris and work and dishes, these precious hours with Becket can't be recovered.

Someone asked me last year what surprised me most about motherhood. I said projectile poop. Which is true. A newborn baby with enough stored up business can actually shoot that business a solid ten feet across a room. Thirty years of babysitting and helping friends with their kids, and somehow, I never knew this.

The second biggest surprise, though, is that I didn't anticipate the goodbyes.

Two years ago yesterday, I left California with a baby who weighed six pounds, had legs like a frog, and pursed his lips together like a duck. Then, one day, I woke up, and he was gone. In his place was another baby, who stopped crying as soon as I sang, loved his swing, and wanted nothing to do with anyone but me.

The following spring, he left us too. His replacement was a fat, happy baby, who got around the room by rolling, turned up his nose at all food but milk, and chewed on his teething Rosary all day long. I adored him. Until one day, I looked around and couldn't find him either. Instead, I found a crawling daddy's boy, obsessed with sticks and wanting to eat everything in sight, from lobster to floor fuzz.

At least three other Tobys have come and gone since then. There was a cruising troublemaker who raced over to the washing machine every time I started a new load, desperate to see his beloved bubbles. There was Daddy's toddling adventure boy, who spent the everlasting spring quarantine rambling through our neighborhood with Chris, stopping every eighteen inches to marvel at another rock or stick. And now there's the boy I came home to last night, who was too busy running after the big kids to give me a hug, talks a mile a minute, and somehow knows the name of every construction vehicle we pass on the way to the hospital.

I've loved saying hello to every new Toby. I look forward

to meeting more. But still, I didn't expect the goodbyes. I didn't realize that you fell in love with a baby who was there one day and gone the next. Nobody told me that each new stage of motherhood is also a little death—the death of the babe that was and the death of the mom you were to them. Growth is good. Progress is a joy. And Toby is always Toby. But I miss the newborn, infant, and baby I knew. I want them all. I want to hold every version of him in my arms all at once. And I don't want to let any of them go.

That, however, is a gift reserved to God alone. He sees every version of us all at once, holds every version of us all at once, loves every version of us all at once. That's why His parenting of us is perfect, and ours always falls short. He sees the whole. We see in part.

Still, I have this dream that someday, in Heaven, when God fully shares His life with us, He'll share that gift too. I pray He'll let us hold in our arms every version of the children we love, and that we'll never have to say goodbye.

Until then, we just have today and a few fleeting moments with the child that is. So, hold onto those moments, Emily. Hold onto those babies. Literally. Every chance you get, every time you can, hold onto them. Be their bed for ten minutes, an hour, two hours, whatever you can spare. And while you hold them, put down the phone from time to time and look at them—at their flushed cheeks, curling eyelashes, and tiny turned-up noses.

This stopping will be hard for you, Emily. You've spent a lifetime rushing about, doing and accomplishing. Sitting in a chair for hours at a stretch, letting counters go unwiped or the deadlines go unmet, isn't your nature. It goes against who you think you are, who you've been told to be. But I promise it's the best thing in the world for you. The dirty countertops and deadlines will always be there. These babies won't. You'll blink and the baby you love will be gone, never to return. And you will weep for him—totally in love with the new child standing before you, but totally bereft for the child that left.

One good thing about being an old mom is that I don't need strangers in Target to tell me how fast it all goes. I already know. I blinked and my friends' babies—babies I held and chased and twirled in circles with—grew up. They go to dances now, drive now, even have babies of their own now. Their little lives fly by so fast, Emily. It won't always feel like it. But this time, with this baby, it's just a moment. It's passing. It's almost gone.

Blessings,
Emily

·∾ঌৡৈ৵·
32

"THIS IS HARD . . .
FOR EVERYONE."

September 5, 2020
Hawthorne House

Dear Emily,
So much for daily letters . . . or even weekly letters. That plan disappeared along with sleep, which I haven't had for almost a month.

Nevertheless, we are home, which is a blessing. Becket was finally released from the hospital on August 10. We left Texas on August 12, and after three days in the car, with me sandwiched between the car seats and covered in an array of bodily fluids, we pulled into our driveway.

It's good to be here, although we're still adjusting. Becket is a love, but his little tummy just doesn't seem ready for food. He spits up constantly—maybe four or five times a feed—and won't be put down for anything. Even diaper changes have him screaming. The only way we can get him to sleep, day or night is on one of us—and by "us" I mostly mean me.

This is hard—legitimately, objectively hard. I find myself living in this weird tension between exhaustion and elation, feeling a half-dozen contradictory emotions all at once. We are so, so grateful to be Becket's parents. He is a gift. We are overwhelmed by the sweetness and beauty of this little man. But we're also overwhelmed by him.

In some moments, I feel guilty saying that. We prayed and worked so hard for Becket, and it seems wrong to feel any emotion other than gratitude. In my more reasonable moments, though, I know that adopting a baby doesn't make raising a baby any less hard. Adoptive or not, I'm still a mom, with a toddler and a newborn. Which is demanding, exhausting, all-consuming work.

There are a million quotes from saints, popes, and writers about the beauty of motherhood. In my head, I know they are true. Motherhood is beautiful. It's holy work. It shapes the world by shaping souls. In the thick of it, though, the beauty can be hard to see. Because no matter how beautiful, holy, and important motherhood is, it's also hard, especially in the season where babies are coming fast and furious, and no one's old enough yet to wipe their own bottoms.

I have only the vaguest idea of what it will be like to have older kids. Some women tell me it's easier. Some say it's just as hard, only in different ways. I'll let you know in another fifteen years. But this? What I'm doing right now? I've never heard a single mother call this season easy.

As a mother of little ones, you are more than their world; you're their sun. You're the light that sustains them, giving them all the nourishment, care, affection, and wisdom they need to grow. You're also the light that helps them discover who they are. Your children learn that they're loveable through your love. They learn that they matter through how much they matter to you. You are their first teacher in love, faith, virtue, manners, movement, language, and the basics of bodily hygiene. The lessons you give them will stay with them for the rest of their lives, for good or for ill. That's terrifying. And overwhelming. And exhausting. You're raising a person who is meant to live forever as a creature greater than the angels or worse than a demon. You're readying them for Heaven or hell. You're forming them for holiness or damnation . . . while also keeping them clean, fed, and out of the washing machine. Never underestimate the Herculean effort required in spending even one hour watching over a toddler with a passion for tight spaces.

As a mother, you can't do any of this work without dying to yourself five hundred times a day—without letting go of your to-do list, surrendering control of your days and nights, and lowering your standards about what a house should look like. You also can't do it without controlling your temper, holding your tongue, and putting down your phone (or setting aside your book or turning off the podcast), so you can be present to your children when they need you.

It might sound easy enough to you now, Emily, but trust me, these deaths are hard. Few of us die them well. Especially today, in a world where so few of us are prepared for this kind of self-denial. As a culture, we invest our energy in telling boys and girls to shoot for the stars, not to die to themselves, so when the time for that dying comes, it feels all the more painful, all the less natural.

Lots of us are also doing this work while trying to help pay the bills and while living on the opposite side of the country from our mothers and sisters. Throw in how much time we spend online, looking at highly curated and edited images of motherhood that bear only the faintest resemblance to the everyday experience of raising actual children, who leak bodily fluids all day long and have stubborn wills of their own, and you have the recipe for even the best of mothers feeling like a failure.

No matter what you see online, though, nobody's experience of motherhood is all blanket-laden beds, matching pajamas, and apple-picking outings. Every mother, at some point, struggles. Every mother, at some point, feels like she's not good enough or wise enough or patient enough or organized enough or happy enough or playful enough or pretty enough or loving enough. Every mother, at some point, also starts to come apart at the seams—as the house falls apart and work deadlines go unmet and sleep deprivation takes hold and paperwork piles up and the emotional or behavioral or relational needs of her child leave her at a complete and utter loss.

I've never met a mother yet, who, at some point, hasn't thrown her hands up in despair and wanted to run for the hills . . . or at least hide out in the bathroom for an inordinate amount of time.

I love the life I'm living now. I wouldn't trade the sleepless nights and endless loads of laundry for even one day in your single shoes. I lived your life, with plenty of freedom, time, and money, for decades. It was a good life. But I prefer this life. There is more laughing in this life, more playing, more dancing, more singing. I am touched, hugged, and kissed more times in a single day than I was in the entirety of my twenties and thirties. I see the purpose of these years. I see the glory. This is the most beautiful kind of hard. But it's still hard.

When these exhausting, crazy, beautiful days come

for you, Emily, remember that it's okay if you need to hide in the bathroom for a while. Every woman does. But while you're hiding, don't think it's because you're doing something wrong. Don't think you're not cut out for motherhood. And definitely don't think it's just you struggling, crying, and feeling confused by the beauty and terror of your days with your babes. You're not doing something wrong. You are doing something right. You are doing hard, holy, sanctifying work, whose fruit will endure forever. And you are not alone. This is life for all of us with little children. This, for this season, is motherhood.

Blessings,
Emily

·⁓ঔৡ⁓·
33

"YOU ARE NOT WHAT YOU DO."

September 12, 2020
Hawthorne House

Dear Emily,

It has been a week. Becket is still not sleeping well at night, still refusing to be anywhere but my arms, and still going through a solid three to four outfits a day thanks to his acid reflux. Toby is handling being a big brother well enough, but it's an adjustment for him, so he's coming into our bed around 1 a.m. and insisting on sleeping there until morning. Which means I am sitting up awake most of the night with Becket sleeping on my chest and Toby glued to my side.

It is beautiful. It is precious. It is a grace to have both these little boys holding so fast to me. It's also exhausting. I can barely remember my name I'm so tired, and everything from writing to laundry is taking three times as long to do . . . if it gets done at all. There is actually more *not* getting done in this house than getting done at this point. Every day, I make a list of things I hope to accomplish, and every day I'm lucky if I can knock off maybe one or two of those things.

Just in case you're wondering, yes, this drives me crazy. I may have grown in all sorts of ways these past twenty years, but I'm still a doer. I crave order and organization and getting everything done when it's supposed to be done. Some days, if I'm not careful, I can start to feel like one big disappointment to myself.

Of all the lessons motherhood will teach you, Emily, this one will be the hardest. You've spent your whole life defining yourself by your accomplishments. You found your identity not just in your intelligence but in your competence. You always have been the girl who gets things done. And not just done, but done better, faster, and more efficiently than anyone else. You don't fail. You exceed expectations. You save the day.

A year from your now, in January of 2002, you will walk away from a slew of impressive job offers in D.C. and go instead to a tiny Catholic university in Ohio. When you do that, you will think you're walking away from that high-octane version of yourself. You pat yourself on the back for caring more about God's will than your resume and tell yourself that your days of being someone who defines herself by what she does are over.

But they aren't over, Emily. Your location changes. Your job title changes. But you don't change. It's true: you don't define yourself by your job, but you still define yourself by what you do. Or, more accurately, how you do what you do. No matter what is is—grad school, working for one of your professors, writing for the university or for yourself, you always expect yourself to be the best. You always expect yourself to succeed. Because that's what you think makes you good, worthy, and loveable. To your family. To your friends. And most of all to God.

If someone asked you, "Does God love you unconditionally?" you would answer yes without hesitation. But deep down, you don't believe it. You are terrified that if you fail, if you aren't doing everything He asks and doing it perfectly, He won't love you, He won't take care of you, He won't stay with you. His disappointment in you will drive Him away.

You don't admit this to yourself for years. Then, along comes motherhood, and it shines a big, bright spotlight on your soul, showing you just how much your identity is wrapped up in doing. Because nothing can blow up "doing" like babies.

Trust me, no matter how early you get up in the morning to pray, the second your fingers touch your Rosary beads, your two-year-old will wake up and start calling for you from his bed. If you schedule an important phone call with a client, the odds are high you will need to cancel that phone call because the sitter will get sick or you will get sick or someone's nap won't go according to plan. And on more days than not, as soon as you start to clean the kitchen or schedule doctor appointments or answer emails, those plans will quickly be upended by a baby who needs to be held, a toddler who finds a Sharpie, an explosive diaper that requires submerging the child immediately in water, or any one of a million possible interruptions that small children can devise. And oh, do they ever devise them.

There is not a baby or toddler on the planet who cares even the littlest bit about what their mothers want to accomplish over the course of a day or a week. Little ones have their own agenda, and it almost always will supersede yours. Thank God for that, Emily. Praise Him for that.

You may not feel like giving thanks in the moment, but

these interruptions, disruptions, and delays are a gift. They are a blessing. Not only do they show you how much you still define yourself by what you do; they also help you start to overcome that. They teach you like nothing else ever has that it's not what you do that matters, but who you are. They help you value being over doing. Because that's what your babies care about. You. Not how many books you write or how much laundry you put away. Just you. Your presence. Your gaze. Your arms.

Babies don't care if you have five hundred thousand followers on Instagram or only five. They just want you to hold them. If you haven't exercised or cleaned the bathroom or scheduled dentist appointments for everyone, they're good with that . . . as long as you'll read *Little Blue Truck* to them fifteen times before noon. Toddlers are not impressed by your job title, your salary, the awards you win, or the accolades you receive . . . unless you are a garbage man, construction worker, or princess. That could get you some cred with the two-year-old crowd. Beyond that, to them, your professional accomplishments pale in comparison to your willingness to clap and marvel at the tower they've built or the picture they've drawn.

Your babies will love you. As you are. In your yoga pants and half-done makeup, with deadlines piling up and your basement looking liking something from an episode of *Hoarders*. They will ask little of you besides your presence and attentiveness. Fruit snacks are appreciated, too, but mostly they will just want you there, eyes on them. God feels something similar.

God doesn't need you to write a dozen books for Him or preach the Gospel to fifty thousand people. He doesn't need you at all. He just loves you, for your sake. He thought you up all on His own. You were an idea in His head before you were a baby in your mother's womb. He loved you then. He loves you now. Your value to Him is not your work or your gifts or your accomplishments. It's not about what you can do for Him. It's about your existence. You bring Him joy because you are.

There's a remarkable passage in Robert Farrar Capon's book *The Supper of the Lamb*, which I think about often these days. He writes:

> [God] likes onions, therefore they are. The fit, the colors, the smell, the tensions, the tastes, the tex-tures, the likes, the shapes are a response, not to some forgotten decree that there may as well be onions as turnips, but to His present delight—His intimate and immediate joy in all you have seen, and in the thousand other wonders you do not even suspect. With Peter, the onion says, Lord, it is good for us to be here. Yes, says God. Tov, Very good.[17]

If that's true of an onion, if God can delight in an onion, marvel at an onion, and choose to hold that onion in existence because of His love for it, how much more true is that of you?

God delights in you. God marvels at you. He holds you in existence in an act of pure, joyful, wondrous love. Some-thing similar can be said of everyone who loves you—your babies, your husband, your family, your friends. They don't love that you do. They love that you are.

Someday, your kids might be proud of what you've

accomplished professionally. Maybe they'll show off a shelf of your books to their children and marvel that Grandma somehow managed to write so much. Or maybe they'll teach your grandchildren and great-grandchildren how to cook your risotto or tell stories about the beauty of the home you made for them. The work you do, as a writer and a homemaker, will be good. You will be proud of it.

But the exact number of books that you write and the speed with which you put laundry away won't be what shapes your children's souls. That's not what will make them healthy, faithful, confident, generous, affectionate, wise, prayerful, loving, and good. That will be grace. And it will be you—you being healthy, you being faithful, you being confident, generous, affectionate, wise, prayerful, loving, and good.

Like I said, I'm still working on getting this understanding out of my head and into my heart. I'm writing in the living room this morning because I can't stand looking at the piles of papers that need sorting in my office. I also will get frustrated later today if the boys refuse to nap and I can't take care of the calls I need to make.

At the same time, I've been doing this long enough to know that the world won't end if I don't get those papers sorted. The phone calls will eventually get made. And someday, me getting stuff done won't hang so heavily on a two-year-old's nap schedule. Seasons for ticking off items on a to-do list will come again. But I won't have one ounce more value then, when that season comes, than I do now. I am not worth more when I do more. *You* are not worth more when you do more. Not to your children. Not to your husband. Not to your friends. And definitely not to God.

You are worth more than an onion. And onions are pretty spectacular.

Blessings,
Emily

34

"MOTHERHOOD MATTERS."

September 19, 2020
Hawthorne House

Dear Emily,

Yesterday, I looked back on these letters on new motherhood. What stood out was how much of me was in them. Unlike my other letters, where I at least tried to hand on some of the wisdom of the saints or teaching of the Church, my letters on motherhood have mostly been my sleep-deprived thoughts and impressions.

I suppose I could dig up some saint quotes to send along. But the fact that these particular letters are so filled with my own thoughts isn't entirely my fault. When it comes to actual Church teaching on motherhood, especially these first all-consuming years, there isn't much. No popes have written encyclicals about how to get your baby to sleep. The *Catechism* doesn't address toddler tantrums. If you want the Church to tell you how you can combat picky eating, you're out of luck. When it comes to motherhood, the Church gives general principles: be open to a child and welcome the child; love, provide, and set a good example for your child; teach your child how to serve, pray, and forgive. For the rest, you're on your own.

Even when it comes to the perennial question of mothers and careers, the Church refrains from telling individual women what to do. In *Familiaris Consortio*, St. John Paul II's encyclical on the family, he says it's a problem when women *have* to leave their young children for the workforce and that "society must be structured in such a way that wives and mothers are not in practice compelled to work outside the home."[18] Beyond that, the Church, at this point in history, gives mothers and fathers the freedom to discern the division of labor inside and outside their home based on their individual circumstances.

There is one teaching about motherhood, however, that the Church has repeated over and over again. Economies have changed, cultures have changed, and expectations of women have changed. But what has remained unchanged is the Church's insistence that the work mothers do in our homes matters. It is, John Paul explains, of "irreplaceable value." He then adds, "The mentality which honors women more for their work outside the home than for their work within the family must be overcome."[19]

I work. I write from home. I can do this because I get up insanely early in the morning (even with a baby) and have a good friend who comes over to help three mornings a week. I am beyond fortunate that I can provide for my family and use my gifts without leaving my home or spending whole days away from my boys. Even when our sitter is here, I can pause my writing for diaper changes, to read to Toby before he naps, and to give hugs when the boys miss Mama.

This is good. I wish this is how it could be for every mother (and fathers, too!). But it's not. And from my position of good fortune, I'm never going to tell other women—especially women whose personal, vocational, and financial circumstances I don't know—that they shouldn't leave the home to work.

At the same time, I know the Church is right. My work as a mother, in the home, is of irreplaceable value. My writing doesn't matter more than my mothering. My writing has value. It's brought grace into my life, and I hope it brings grace to others, too. But I have no idea how much grace. When I write, I don't know if anyone listens to me. But I know Toby and Becket listen to me.

Every day, my sons see me trying to live the truths behind the words I write. Their eyes are always on me, as I cook, clean, snuggle, and play. Everything I do in this house is a lesson to them. How I look at them. How I kiss their bellies and toes when changing their diapers. How I dress them, feed them, chase them, pray with them, clean up after them, read to them, stop my work to hold them, marvel at their smallest achievements, and pick them up in the night when they cry. They see it all, with my every word and action communicating to them their worth, their importance, their dignity.

Someday, Emily, in your home, from you, your children will learn what it means to be a human person, made in the image of God. They will learn the obligations we have to God and to one another. They will learn what it means to serve and be served, give and receive, forgive and be forgiven. They also will learn who God is from you. Not so much by what you tell them about Him, but much more by how you love them.

You (and their father) will be the first image of God in your boys' lives. They will come to understand God's love through your love. They will learn about His wisdom through your wisdom. They will experience His mercy, His generosity, and His faithfulness through your mercy, generosity, and faithfulness. The witness you give to God through your actions will shape how they see God for the rest of their lives, for better or worse.

This is one reason why the Church calls the family the domestic church. Because in our homes, with our families, we are formed for Heaven or Hell. From our parents, we learn to be a gift to others or to use others. We learn to welcome people in or shut people out. We learn to love and serve, or we learn to hate and fear. No matter what happens when they leave home, the lessons children learn in the domestic church will stay with them forever. Almost nothing else will help or hinder them more than how you live together in your home and how you love them in your home.

And it really is you who will have this power. Other writers can write what you write. But in your home, with your children, you are one of a kind. No babysitter, no teacher, no childcare provider can fill the irreplaceable role you have in your children's lives.

It is easy to lose sight of this. We've already talked about how hard this early stage of motherhood is, but it bears repeating: When you become a mother, the responsibility will exhaust and overwhelm you. The daily work of caring for them is so much harder than the work of writing. And writing is not easy! My brain always feels broken after a few hours wrestling with a text. But my body, my brain, and my spirit feel broken after a few hours wrestling with a toddler who won't listen and a baby who won't stop crying and doing it all on only a few hours of interrupted sleep.

To make it even more difficult, the rewards of the work of motherhood aren't immediately evident. Yes, there are the hugs and "I love you, Mamas," but there aren't a steady stream of "thank-yous" for diaper changes, lunches served, toy rooms picked up, and laundry washed. You don't get praised for putting your toddler down for a nap. More likely you get hit in the head with a sippy cup. And there are no pay raises for prayers said before meals, pleases and thank-yous enforced, and effective discipline carried out. You don't get a paycheck at all!

It can take years or decades to see the fruit of your labors as a mom. And while you wait, you often have no idea if you're doing it right. You regularly will feel like you are failing, because the benchmarks aren't clear. The goalposts move. Different children need different things at different times. Different children mature, develop, and meet milestones at different times. No motherhood playbook exists that applies without fail to every mother and every child.

Because of this, your professional work will often feel more fulfilling. The rewards it brings are measurable and immediate. At work, you know you matter. At work, you can see you're accomplishing what you set out to do. And so the temptation for you, like for many other women (and men!), will be to prioritize your career over your children; to think that you are irreplaceable at work but replaceable in the home; and to decide you should give the best of your time, energy, and talents to the work that helps many people, not the work that helps only two.

G. K. Chesterton dismissed that idea out of hand a century ago, asking:

How can it be a large career to tell other people's children about the Rule of Three, and a small career to tell one's own children about the universe? How can it be broad to be the same thing to everyone, and narrow to be everything to someone? No; a woman's function is laborious, but because it is gigantic, not because it is minute.[20]

Like with most things, Chesterton knew what he was talking about. At best, Emily, your work will touch people's lives along the margins. It might help them with a particular struggle or at a particular point in time. It might help them in big and important ways. But it won't shape the whole of their life. For your boys, though, that's exactly what your work as a mother will do.

The long, exhausting, seemingly thankless days and nights you spend with Toby and Becket will lay the foundation for how they understand themselves, the world, and God. How you love and care for them will be the touchstone by which every person and every event for the rest of their lives is measured. For your boys, your motherhood will be everything. To your boys, you will be everything. Well, you and Chris will be everything. His fatherhood matters, too.

And yes, your work as a writer can teach Toby and Becket important lessons about answering God's call in the world. But only if you are just as faithful in answering God's call to mother them. The extent to which your children value your work will ultimately be determined by the extent to which they feel valued by you.

Unlike the books you write, the fruit of your motherhood will last forever, Emily. So, no matter where God has you working or what He has you doing, try to make sure the order of your days and years reflects that. Don't ever doubt the importance of the time, energy, and love you're investing in your family. Don't undersell it. Don't undervalue it. Your writing will matter. To your family, to you, to the Church. But your motherhood will matter more—eternally more.

Blessings,
Emily

On Prayer

.❧.
35

"CAST YOUR EYES
ON JESUS."

September 22, 2020
Hawthorne House

Dear Emily,

Annnndddd . . . the locusts have arrived. They're all over Africa now. So, it's time to talk prayer.

I had hoped to save these letters for a week . . . or a month . . . where Becket was letting me sleep for more than twenty-five consecutive minutes. But I probably shouldn't delay any longer. The zombies may be here any minute.

What I have to say about prayer won't be much compared to what could be said. Whole libraries could be filled with books written about prayer. The Church's teachings on prayer are vast and deep. So, in the years to come, read everything you can by St. John of the Cross, St. Teresa of Avila, St. Francis de Sales, St. Elizabeth of the Trinity, and (for a more modern summation of those giants) Ralph Martin and Fr. Thomas Dubay. They will give you a far deeper understanding of prayer than I can in these few short pages. For now, I'll just stick to the essentials, starting with the nature of prayer.

Prayer is easy to overcomplicate. Some people get hung up on the words of prayer and think they're only praying well if they use set prayers given to us by the Church. Other people would like to share their heart more freely with God but aren't sure how. So, they don't say anything at all.

Prayer, though, is about so much more than words. At its most basic, prayer is just giving our attention to God, focusing on Him rather than on our kids, our work, or what's on our phone. Sometimes, when we give God our attention, we talk to Him. Sometimes we listen to Him. Sometimes we read about Him or think about Him or simply sit with Him. Always, though, the heart of prayer consists of directing our hearts and minds toward Him. St. John Paul II once described prayer this way, writing:

> All harm comes to us from not keeping our eyes fixed on [Jesus]. If we were to look at nothing else but the way, we would soon arrive. Remember Jesus, close to your side . . . Get used to this practice. Get used to it. I'm not asking you to do anything more than look at Him.[21]

Jesus loves you. And just like we want the people we love to pay attention to us, Jesus wants the people He loves to pay attention to Him. Unlike us, though, He doesn't want our attention because He needs it or because it makes Him feel good. He wants it because we need it. He made us for Himself. He holds us in being every second of every day, and the more attention we pay to Him, the more readily we can live the lives He wants us to live. Prayer connects us to the source of our life, strengthening us, healing us, and transforming us. That's the heart of prayer: attentiveness in emotion and thought to the One who knows us and loves us.

Now, if you want to go deeper, there are more ways to think about prayer and classify prayer. There is ascetical prayer (prayer we initiate) and mystical prayer (prayer God initiates). There is vocal prayer (us talking to God) and mental prayer (God talking to us). There is meditative prayer (allowing God to illuminate our intellects and reason as we study sacred words or objects) and contemplative prayer (allowing God to illuminate our emotions as we experience a wordless union with Him).

All these forms of prayer matter. All are important. All help you draw closer to Him. But prayer still starts with simply looking at Jesus. And that is what you need to work on, Emily. You need to cultivate an awareness of Jesus's presence. You need to know He is always close to you, always interested in you, always loving you. The more you realize this, the easier it becomes to share your heart with Him and hear Him speaking in the quiet of your soul.

One of the simplest ways to cultivate this awareness is to take John Paul II's advice literally. Hang a crucifix in every room of your house. Find some pictures of Jesus and hang those up, too. Be the Catholic who has a Rosary hanging from your rearview mirror. Or who wears a Rosary bracelet everywhere you go. Surround yourself with images of Our Lord so that when you get stressed, angry, scared, or confused, you can cast your actual eyes in His "direction." Do the same when you're happy, excited, or grateful for some little gift that has come your way.

The more you look to Jesus in these moments, the easier it becomes to share your heart with Him—to whisper, "Thank you!" "I love you!" "Why?" and "How?" It also becomes easier to listen to Him—to sit with Him, knowing He is there, and let the Holy Spirit direct your thoughts and emotions.

There won't always be images of Jesus wherever you go. John Paul II's advice isn't quite as literal as mine. He's advising you to look at Jesus with your interior gaze—the mind and the heart's eye. And you should. Do that. Do it always. That's the best way of following St. Paul's directive to "Pray always." Cultivating that interior gaze, however, takes practice. So many shiny things exist in the world to distract us and confuse us. This is why I advise you to start with the literal. The more you develop the habit of casting your actual eyes on Jesus in moments of need, crisis, joy, and sorrow, the easier it becomes to tune out the distractions of the world and cast your mind's eye on Him wherever you are, whatever you're doing, and hear His voice.

As always, there's more to say, but I only have thirty minutes of babysitting left this morning, and if I don't use it to shower, no shower is happening today! Until tomorrow!

All my prayers,
Emily

"DON'T TREAT JESUS LIKE A SHORT-ORDER COOK."

September 24, 2020
Hawthorne House

Dear Emily,

Two days ago (although it feels like only yesterday to me, since I haven't slept in forty-eight hours), we talked about the nature of prayer and how, at its most basic, prayer is directing our minds and hearts to God. It's the most fundamental way we pursue a relationship with Jesus Christ. It's how we get to know Him.

For His part, Jesus doesn't need to get to know us. He knows us already, inside and out, from head to toe, from first day to last. But no matter how much Scripture or theology we read, we can never know Him unless we pray. In prayer, when we look at Him and He looks at us, we encounter His heart. We see the goodness, mercy, justice, power, wisdom, and majesty at which His creation only hints. Just like we can never really know a person without spending time with them and talking with them, we can't really know Jesus without spending time with Him and talking with Him. This happens in prayer.

But what do we talk to Jesus about? What do we say when we sit down before Him? Can we just say the prayers we memorized in school: the "Our Father" or a "Hail Mary"?

What about going to church on Sunday and praying the words of the Mass? Can we do only that and call it good? No. Those prayers are good. They're great. They're holy words given to us by Jesus and the saints. You should pray them. But they're not sufficient for developing an intimate relationship with Jesus. Moreover, if we're not careful, we can fall into the trap of just praying the words we think Jesus wants us to pray, and never praying what we need to pray.

What's also not sufficient is what you tend to do, Emily: approach Jesus daily with a litany of requests. You, like a lot of people, treat the Creator of the Universe as if He exists to serve you—to make you stronger, smarter, happier, and more successful. You ask and you ask and you ask, turning to Him daily in your need, but rarely taking your conversations with Him beyond that. It's good to ask for what you need. He tells us to do this. But again, it's not sufficient. Jesus is not your genie, and He didn't create you and call you to a relationship with Himself simply so you could get the help you need meeting deadlines or finding a husband.

You have to work on treating Jesus less like a short-order cook and more like your Beloved, the one for whom you were made.

Think of how you would talk to a boyfriend. You wouldn't spend all your time together doing nothing but telling him what you need and asking him for things. Not if you wanted the relationship to last. No, you would tell your boyfriend you love him. You would thank him for all the good he does. You would ask for his forgiveness when you screwed up. And you would praise him for all that was wonderful about him.

Jesus is not your boyfriend. He is your Savior. But the fundamentals of conversation in a loving relationship remain the same, whether we're talking about the cute guy at work or the Incarnate Word.

When you pray, you need to tell Jesus you love Him and adore Him (a form of prayer the Church calls Adoration and Blessing). You also should thank Him for all the good gifts He sends your way—your family, your friends, your home, the food in your belly, and the sun on your face (these are Prayers of Thanksgiving). You should praise Jesus for all that's wonderful about Him—His justice, mercy, creativity, love, kindness, and a hundred other holy attributes (Prayers of Praise). And, when you sin, when you hurt yourself or someone else, you should ask His forgiveness (a Prayer of Contrition), because all sin, ultimately, is a sin against God.

It's okay to ask for more than forgiveness, of course. Jesus does wants you to ask Him for what you need and what you desire, too (Prayers of Petition). He also wants you to think of people besides yourself and ask Him to help others—to heal them or strengthen them or bless them. When we do this, we're interceding for someone (praying Prayers of Intercession).

These are the five basic forms of prayer as outlined in the *Catechism*: Blessing and Adoration, Petition and Contrition, Intercession, Thanksgiving, and Praise. You don't have to include all five forms every time you pray any more than you would say all those things at once every time your boyfriend walked in the door. But you do need to make sure you're getting them all in over the course of a day. Never let a day go by without telling Jesus you love Him. Never let the sun go down without examining your conscience and asking Jesus for forgiveness (and getting to Confession on the regular). Tell Jesus the desires of your heart when you long for something and ask Him to grant them according to His will. Intercede for others daily. Thank Him constantly. And marvel at His goodness without ceasing.

A strong and healthy prayer life is a rich and varied prayer life. With the Church, pray the Mass and the Divine Office (I'm a big fan of the abbreviated Office in the *Magnificat*). With the Scriptures, pray the Psalms. Meditate on the Rosary. Sit before Jesus in Adoration and contemplate His holy face, hidden in the Eucharist. Sing the ancient hymns of the Church, lifting your heart and mind to God as you lift your voice to Him. But most important—daily, hourly, in every possible moment—talk to Jesus in your own words. Go to Him again and again throughout the day, in times of joy and sorrow, stress and want, adoring, petitioning, interceding, thanking, apologizing, and praising. Those conversations are the heartbeat of all relationships, including your relationship with God.

Blessings,
Emily

37

"WHISPER TO JESUS IN THE CHAOS."

September 29, 2020
Hawthorne House

Dear Emily,

Okay, we are officially three letters into this conversation on prayer, and I have a confession to make: I feel like a bit of an idiot giving you this advice.

When it comes to prayer, I'm just a baby. There are countless holier, wiser, more prayerful people than I from whom you can learn. I haven't experienced the depths of mystical prayer or gone into ecstatic trances. I could give you the technical definition of "the prayer of union," but I'm as personally familiar with that kind of prayer as I am with the Queen of England. Heck, I'm barely doing the basics these days. I haven't had time for Eucharistic Adoration in ages, and when I get through one mystery of the Rosary without my mind wandering to what emails I haven't returned, I feel like I deserve a prize.

So, why these letters and not just a page of book recommendations on prayer?

I'm not sure. Maybe because someday, you won't want to hear from a spiritual master about prayer. You'll want to hear from someone like me. Someone who has barely slept for months, who has babies attached to her twenty-two hours a day, laundry piled up in her bedroom, dishes in the sink, work deadlines looming, and a pile of paperwork on her desk that she's more than a little scared to sort through. Like 95 percent of the female population over the age of eighteen, I'm drowning. And before you know it, you will be drowning, too. Life is going to come at you fast, and when you're juggling work and family, housekeeping and friendships, aging parents and difficult in-laws, the advice on prayer that cloistered nuns and monks have to give can seem a little useless. It's not! It's not useless at all. But during certain seasons of life, it will seem that way because it's so far removed from your experience of daily life. You will find yourself wondering how on earth you're supposed to find an hour every morning to sit quietly with the Lord when you've got a small human being in bed with you who wakes up as soon as you even contemplate getting up to pray. Or you'll be asking yourself how you can get to daily Mass when your parish schedules it for the very hour you need to get to work?

During some seasons in life, daily Mass and lengthy quiet times with the Lord are possible. During other seasons, they're not, and no amount of wishing or willpower can change that. And when we can't do what we used to do or what we'd like to do—when we can't get to daily Mass or a daily Holy Hour or spend an hour reading Scripture and journaling in the morning—the temptation is not to pray at all. It's to put conversations with God on the back burner, along with concerts, dinners out, and quiet nights reading by the fire, thinking, "I'll do that again someday."

But you don't need God someday. You need Him today. You need to talk to Him now and listen to Him now and call upon Him now in the midst of your crazy, chaotic, spit-up-laden life. (Okay, actually that's my life. Not yours quite yet. But it will be your life at the end of the world, so the point holds.)

How do you do that, then? How do you pray when you can't pray like so many saints say to pray?

You find new saints to listen to—like St. Francis de Sales. In his classic work on Christian spirituality, *Introduction to the Devout Life*, he advises:

> Aspire then frequently to God . . . by short but ardent dartings of your heart; admire His beauty; invoke His aid; cast yourself in spirit at the foot of the cross; adore His Goodness; address Him frequently on your salvation; give your soul to Him a thousand times a day; fix your interior eye upon His sweetness; stretch out your hand as a little child to its father, that He may conduct you . . . plant Him in your soul like a standard; and make a thousand sorts of different motions of your heart, to enkindle the love of God.[22]

That's how I'm praying today. As I walk down the stairs, baby in one arm, the toddler's hand in the other, I whisper, "Jesus, thank you." When I sit down to write after another night without sleep, I quickly beg, "Jesus, I'm so tired. Help me." When I snap at Chris as he walks out the door in the morning, I close my eyes and say, "God, forgive me." When I make the mistake of checking Twitter or watching the evening news, I stare at the picture in my living room of Jesus weeping over Jerusalem, and pray, "Lord, have mercy on us, we know not what we do." And when something breaks, when a baby makes us late for Mass yet again, when I miss a deadline, when I'm tempted to cry or shout or throw something across the room, I take a deep breath and say, "Jesus, I love you. Praise you, Lord. Bless you."

These prayers aren't going to have me bilocating anytime soon. But they are doing something more important. They're keeping me in conversation with God. In a season of life where busyness threatens to drive God out, they invite Him in. When a thousand different demands on my time make it easy to neglect God, they keep Him close. When the greatest spiritual temptation I face is to forget about God in the chaos of my life, they remind me that He is with me in the chaos, that He is with me every blessed second, dwelling in what St. Elizabeth of the Trinity described as "the sanctuary of my soul," loving me, guiding me, strengthening me, consoling me.

These little aspirations aren't my only prayers these days. Despite the Baby Who Will Not Sleep, I manage to pray my Rosary most mornings and, when I have a little more time, I review the day's Scripture readings. At night, Chris and I hold the babies while offering prayers for the people we know who need them. We pray before meals. We try to pray the Angelus at noon and six. We go to Mass on Sundays and soak in what grace we can. And about once a day, when all the stars align, I sit down wherever I can and seek out Jesus's face in the room—on a crucifix or painting or statue. We look at each other in the quiet. Then, a baby calls, and I return to whispering to Jesus in the chaos, binding myself to Him in the midst of our madness.

I'm not falling into any ecstatic trances yet. But maybe

someday these little whispers will make that possible. St. Francis de Sales says they could, noting that without them, "no one can lead a true contemplative life, and the active life will be but imperfect where it is omitted: without it rest is but indolence, labor but weariness—therefore I beseech you to adopt it heartily, and never let it go."[23]

This insane season won't last forever. Seasons never do. Before I know it, everyone will be sleeping through the night, including me, and there will be time enough for rising before the sun to spend an hour with Jesus. But, here, now, this is what I can do. This is what all of us drowning people can do. And it helps.

All my love,
Emily

·~~~·
38

"GOD IS NEVER SILENT."

October 7, 2020
Hawthorne House

Dear Emily,

A lot of people are praying today. Some are praying for loved ones. Others are praying for our country. There also are those praying for Jesus to come again. I think I'm in the third camp.

I fear more people aren't praying, though, than are. Either because they never have prayed or because they've given up. They prayed, and God said nothing back. Or they prayed and received the consolations they sought, but then those stopped. No more consolations came. God went silent. So they went silent in return.

God's silence—or I should say, seeming silence—is a problem you will wrestle with in the coming years. Because one day He will seem silent to you, too. You have some lonely decades ahead of you, Emily—decades where you long to share your home and your life with another and decades where you long to carry babies in your womb and in your arms. You will beg God for those gifts, only to have another year go by without receiving them. You will write about God, serve God, praise God, thank God, and seemingly do everything you're supposed to do for God, only to be greeted by a deafening silence when you go to Him in prayer.

Why does this happen? And how do you make sense of it?

Before I answer that question, I should make one thing clear. Our God is many things, but a bad communicator is not one of them. God is an excellent communicator. There's no one better. He has been doing it, literally, forever.

From all eternity, God the Father has been communicating everything He is and has to God the Son, who, in turn, has been receiving everything the Father has to give, and then giving it right back. And that exchange of love and life? That communication of being? It is so complete, so real, that it too is a person. It's the Holy Spirit.

God doesn't just communicate; He is communication. To communicate Himself, to communicate who He is, is an essential part of God's nature.

God's communication skills, however, aren't confined to the inner life of the Trinity. God doesn't work that way. God's actions in human history, what He does in time, always reflect who God is from all eternity. God is consistent, in time and out. Accordingly, since the world began, He has been communicating on earth as He has in Heaven.

We know this from the Bible, which tells us that God created everything through His Word. He spoke creation into being, and now everything in that creation, from mountains and skies, to broccoli stalks and bumblebees, reflects something of Him. The world is a constant act of communication from God to us.

As time went on, God communicated directly with human beings. He walked in the Garden with Adam and Eve. He called out to Noah. He made a covenant with Abraham. He met Moses on a mountaintop. And He spoke to David and all of Israel through His prophets. Then, to make sure we all knew what He'd said to those people, He inspired men and women to write down those conversations and what He wanted humanity to know about Himself.

Even that wasn't enough communication for God, though. He took His communication with humanity to a whole new level, when the Word of God took on flesh, was born of a woman, and walked among us. In Jesus Christ, God revealed Himself completely and perfectly to the world. He didn't just tell us who He was; He showed us. He showed us by teaching us, forgiving us, healing us, and dying for us.

Then, after Jesus returned to the Father, God kept communicating with us through the Church He established, the sacraments He gave us, and the saints He made.

All of which is to say, God is constantly communicating. He never stops. He never goes silent. God can't not communicate. It's who He is. It just doesn't always feel that way to us.

In the years to come, you will experience times in your walk with God where you hear His Word loud and clear, where consolations flood your heart in prayer, and where God is so obviously there. You also will experience times when God's presence isn't obvious. You will pray and pray, but hear nothing. You will look for consolations where you used to find them—in Adoration, prayer, the sacraments— but no consolation will come. Even Scripture won't seem alive anymore, and you will start to wonder if God has forgotten you or if He's even really there.

No matter how silent God seems, though, Emily, He is always there. He could never forget you. And this season of quiet is normal. Every disciple of Jesus experiences it at least once, and usually many times. Even the great saints walk through seasons where God seems silent and far away.

Catherine of Siena, for example, once reproached Jesus for not making an appearance while she did battle with demons—literal, visible demons. "Lord, where were you when my heart was filled with such terrible bitterness?" she asked.

His answer? "I was in your heart. It was my presence which caused the sorrow and bitterness which I know you felt when the devils raged around you. And my grace guarded your heart so that you did not give in to the temptations of the demons."[24]

Now, at times, when God seems silent, the issue is on our end. We humans have a tendency to tune Him out when we don't want to hear what He has to say. Many other times, though, God's seeming silence is for our good. Through the quiet, He helps us grow in faith and spiritual maturity.

God does not want us to become spiritual consolation junkies, always needing a fix of comfort or assurance, nor does He want us to remain immature Christians, always needing constant direction about what to do and where to go. Instead, God wants us to have a mature faith that can withstand trials, suffering, and persecution.

He also wants us to exercise prudence, justice, temperance, and fortitude. He desires that we put our knowledge of Him and His ways to work in the world. He wants us to do what all His communicating with us has been forming us to do.

Remember, God is a Father. And a good father never

wants to buy his child's affection with toys and treats. He wants the child to love him as he is, not for what he gives him. Likewise, no dad wants to hound his child's every move every day of their life, telling them when to go to bed, when to eat, and when to go to the bathroom. If a parent has to do that with a normal, healthy child, they have failed as a parent.

Because of that, God gives us spiritual dry spells, where our faith and hope in Him are stretched, tested, and strengthened. He also gives us seasons where choices are put before us, where there's no clear and obvious direction from Him, so we have to integrate all that we know and believe into making those choices.

If we persevere during these seasons, though, if we hold fast to Him and what we know to be true, these will turn out to be some of the most fruitful seasons of our life. These are the seasons that make us saints. They are a gift, even though they don't always feel much like it at the time.

So, that brings us to the question of how we endure these gifts. What do we do when God seems to go silent?

This letter has already gotten way too long, and I don't trust that Becket's nap will last much longer. So, we'll save that for tomorrow . . . if, God willing, the baby naps.

Blessings,
Emily

·⚬ℓℯ⚬·
39
"IN THE SILENCE, WE DISCOVER THE STRENGTH OF OUR FAITH AND OUR LOVE."

October 8, 2020
Hawthorne House

Dear Emily,

The baby naps! So, I write (and pray for the soul of the person who invented the baby swing).

Now, where were we? God's silence, right? More specifically, what do you do when God seems absent? How do you trust Him when you pray but hear only silence in return?

As I mentioned yesterday, we first have to be honest with ourselves and make sure that we are not the problem—that we are not stubbornly clinging to some sin or bad habit. We have to ask ourselves if God is talking to us plenty and we're not doing the listening.

If the answer to that question is no, it's not us, then the first thing we need to do is practice relying on what we know to be true—about God and about the sanctifying grace that dwells within us. This means we have to keep talking to God. We have to keep praying, sharing our hearts, going to Mass, and sitting before Him, trusting that He is listening and always wants to hear what we have to say. We also have to keep listening for Him. Remember, God is never silent. He is always speaking to us through His Word in Sacred Scripture, in the Church's Liturgy, through the teaching authority of the Church, and through His saints. If you are struggling or in doubt, rely on all the ways God has already made His will clear. He has given us an overabundance of guidance *and* the ability to use common sense to apply that guidance to our situation. He expects us to use both when making decisions.

That's the first thing that can help during times when God seems silent—to remember that His silence is only ever seeming. The second is to pray what I call the Litany of the Hidden God.

This litany isn't a litany of praise. It's a litany of gratitude. It helps us recall all the good God brought out of our suffering in the past. When I pray it, I name every difficult time in my life—when we were struggling with infertility, my single years, when I worked a difficult job, junior high—then list all the gifts that came during and because of those times: friendships, work, travel, spiritual graces, wisdom, babies. As I recall those gifts, I thank God for each one. The more desperate I feel, the longer the litany gets. But it always works.

Recalling concretely how God has blessed me and guided me in the past, even when I couldn't feel Him, helps me trust He is with me in the present. It also reminds me that God does indeed know what He's doing. He has a plan, and it's good.

So, when you're struggling to find God in your present, try looking for Him in your past. Name the blessings

He poured out during times of struggle—blessings you wouldn't have without those struggles. Then give thanks. If it helps, write it all out. Stick the litany on your mirror or in your planner. Glance at it often. Meditate upon it. Pray it.

As you do, the hidden God will emerge from the shadows and reveal Himself to you, reminding you that He is there and that He's not going anywhere. He is leading you through this present darkness and will keep leading you until there is no more darkness, only light.

Lastly, keep in mind that in every marriage, every friendship, every relationship, there are times of conversation and times of silence. There are times when we talk and listen to one another and times when we just look at one another or walk alongside each other.

Those times of silence, of looking, of walking, aren't less intimate than the times of talking. They are more intimate. They are when the truth about the other and the truth about the relationship are revealed. We often learn more about ourselves and our feelings for another in quiet than we learn anywhere else. This is just as true of our relationship with God.

When God seems silent, He is still there. He is still looking at you. He is still loving you. The question is, What will you do? Do you love God enough and trust Him enough to sit with Him in the quiet? Do you really want Him, or do you just want the consolations He gives you? Have you been listening to God and learning from Him so that your mind is growing ever more conformed to His, or is the world's voice the one you still hear?

That's what you discover in the silence: the strength of

your faith and the strength of your love.

You also discover that if you hold fast to what you know and what you believe, God will bless you. In time, He will strengthen your faith and love so that when He speaks again, His word touches you in a whole new way.

Don't fear the silence, Emily. Don't take it as a sign that God has forgotten you. Instead, welcome it as a sign of God's confidence in you—a sign that you are ready for more: more faith, more love, and more intimacy with Him.

Blessings,
Emily

·ᘓᕊᘐ·
40

"ASK GOD FOR
WHAT HE WANTS."

October 14, 2020
Hawthorne House

Dear Emily,

This has been another hard week. Not because of pandemics or politics or protests, but because so many good people I know are enduring their own personal Calvary. An old acquaintance from grad school lost his son. A young boy for whom half the Catholic world seemed to be praying passed away. And a family we know that has been going through the adoption process for years got another no about a possible baby last night. All these families are good families, prayerful families with prayerful friends. God's no to them doesn't make sense.

Like God's seeming silence, this problem of unanswered prayers is something with which you will wrestle over the next twenty years. Especially because it seems to fly in the face of Jesus's promise: "Whatever you ask in my name, I will do it, that the Father may be glorified in the Son" (John 14:13). That sounds pretty straightforward. But we all know that's not how it works out.

Times without number, we ask and don't receive. We pray for spouses and babies that never come. We pray for healings that never happen. We pray for hurricanes to change course that don't. A million prayers a day, and maybe more, don't result in the answer we sought.

What are we to make of that?

Not surprisingly, smart, holy people have come up with all sorts of answers to that question. Some, for example, point out that as fallen creatures, we often ask for the wrong things—for things that aren't good for us—and so God, who is a loving Father, says no. Which makes sense. Others have noted that multiple people often pray for the same gift. Two men pray for the love of the same woman or two women pray for the same job, and God can't give all those people exactly what they want because it's a logical impossibility. This also makes sense.

Then, of course, there are those who remind us that God's no to our prayers often isn't a no. It's a "not yet." This will be the case with you, during all the years when you pray for Chris. It seemed like God was saying "no," but it was "not now." It's also true to say that God often answers our prayers in a deeper way than we intend for Him to do. For instance, we pray for healing for a child lying in a hospital bed, unable to talk or walk after a fall. And God does heal her. He heals her soul. He perfects it through her silent suffering and then calls her to Himself, where she can be forever whole, in body and soul, with Him. That's a better answer than the one for which we prayed. But it's not the answer we wanted, so it feels unanswered.

I could go on. All the best and holiest minds have wrestled with this problem, so no shortage of answers exists. Occasionally, these answers can be helpful. When you're the one who has the unanswered prayer on your hands, however, the answers can feel like splitting hairs. Again,

Jesus said all we had to do was ask. He promised He would answer our prayers. He didn't put a bunch of technical qualifications on that promise. So, what gives?

I don't know. I'm not a saint. I'm not a mystic. I'm not a Doctor of the Church. All I can tell you is how God has worked through some of my unanswered prayers.

Let's start with Chris and the nine years I waited for him to move forward. The wait was excruciating. It was maddening. But it brought me to my knees. Longing for what I didn't have and asking God why kept me close to the Lord during a time when I might otherwise have been tempted to wander far from Him.

More fundamentally, all those years of praying taught me who I am. Or, more accurately, who I am not. They taught me that I am not God. This should have been obvious, but it wasn't. Not to me. It's not to you yet, either. You are tenacious, Emily. You are strong willed. You get things done. So, it's easy for you to fall into the trap of thinking you are in control. You believe if you just exert enough effort, you can get the result you want. But with Chris, you couldn't. I couldn't. I couldn't force a relationship with him. I couldn't wrestle God into it or wrestle Chris into it. I couldn't control the situation.

The more I came to see this, the more I came to understand how little I am, how little I know, and how foolish it is to try to wrestle the all-knowing, all-loving God into giving me something that might not be good for me. So, at some point, I stopped wrestling. I continued to pray my novenas and share my heart with the Lord, but I also started telling Him that what I wanted most was what He wanted. "Change my heart if this isn't what you want for me," I prayed. "Not my will, but yours," I said again and again.

And over time, the more I prayed that, the more I realized that the person I wanted the most wasn't Chris; it was Jesus. I didn't want the prizes, rewards, miracles, healings, or spouses He could hand out. I didn't want what He could do for me. I just wanted Him. Which is the greatest gift God gave me during that time of unanswered prayers: a desire for the Giver of all gifts that exceeded my desire for the gifts. He changed my desires. That changed my prayers.

This doesn't mean my desire to marry Chris went away: it didn't. It also doesn't mean I stopped sharing with God my desire to be a wife or a mother; I didn't. But I did start making every prayer subject to God's will. My prayers changed. I changed. And eventually, the situation changed. That, however, led to another unanswered prayer.

During the first year of our struggle with infertility, I slipped back into my old ways of wrestling with God, demanding a baby, not understanding why He wasn't answering my prayer. But then I remembered the lessons I learned during that decade of praying for Chris and went back to concluding every prayer for a baby with "not my will, but yours." The more I prayed those words, the more I meant those words. And God responded to them, helping me to make peace with infertility, opening my heart to adoption, and ultimately answering my prayers for children in a way more beautiful, joyful, and miracle-filled than I could have imagined.

All that being said, the problem of unanswered prayers remains a mystery to me. I don't know why some women lose their husbands and others get to keep them. I don't understand why some children grow up safe, secure, and loved, while others endure horrific abuse. I don't get why cancer and car accidents and freak falls rob some people of their loved ones despite the prayers of thousands of faithful people. I don't know why Jesus seems to say yes to some prayers and no to others.

But all my years of going to God in prayer have taught me that He loves each and every one of us more than we can possibly imagine. They've taught me that He wants more for us than we want for ourselves. And they've taught me that He is more than capable of giving us exactly what we need when we need it. Prayer taught me trust, and that gave me the ability to have my deepest prayer be "Not my will but yours."

So that's the best advice I have to give you about unanswered prayers, Emily. Don't ever be afraid to share your heart with the Lord. Don't stop asking Him for what your heart desires. Go to Him again and again with your needs and your wants, your fears and your worries. But don't just ask God for what you want. Ask God for what He wants. Ask Him to open your eyes to His plan for you. Ask Him to conform your heart to His. Ask Him to fill you with His desires and make them the desires of your heart.

Will God's "not yet" through all those years of waiting for Chris be easy to take? No. But I can tell you this: Seeing the marriage we have now, a marriage that was built on friendship and has flourished in maturity, I am so grateful for that "not yet." It's one of the reasons we have the marriage we do.

And the babies? Words can't express how grateful I am for infertility. It's the heaviest cross I've ever carried, but without it, I wouldn't have my two boys. I wouldn't be Toby and Becket's mom. And that's about the saddest thing I can think of. I am so glad God didn't answer those desperate prayers of mine in 2016 and 2017 to conceive and instead answered my prayers in 2018 and 2020 to adopt.

And maybe that's the answer to the problem of unanswered prayers. Maybe Jesus answers every prayer we pray in the way we would want it to be answered if we saw what He saw and knew what He knew. Maybe He who dwells in eternity, outside of time, takes into account not just the prayers we pray in the moment but the prayers we pray throughout our entire life, in this world and the next. Maybe He grants us the deepest desires of our everlasting hearts, not just the fleeting desires we have at one moment in time.

Again, it's a mystery. But one day we will see. One day we will understand. For now, we're called to simply trust that what Jesus promises, Jesus means.

Love,
Emily

The Last Things

i

·∾ໄৡ∾·
41

"DO THE DUTY OF THE MOMENT."

October 19, 2020
Hawthorne House

Dear Emily,

At the end of our days, the Catholic Church teaches that every human person must reckon with the same realities. She calls these the "Four Last Things": Death, Judgement, Heaven, and Hell. We all will die. We all will meet Christ the Judge. And we all will enter into the eternity which we freely chose through our actions in the world.

I don't know when my last days will be. I don't know when I'll need to reckon with these realities. But I've been thinking a great deal about them lately—not so much about death or Heaven or Hell exactly, but more about how the relationships and attitudes we cultivate now, in this life, prepare us for this reckoning. What equips us to face death with courage and grace? What virtues can help us live now in a way that anticipates the eternity we desire? How do we see ourselves when we stand before Christ?

These are big questions, and I'm still wrestling with them. I'll try to share what I'm thinking, though, in these last few letters to you. I'll start today by talking about my laundry room.

Not what you were expecting, right?

It's true. Laundry rooms don't usually come up in discussions about the end of all things. Unless it's the end of all baby socks. Not the end of life or life as we know it, though. Nevertheless, my laundry room is indeed helping me answer one of the great questions of the ages: How, in light of our death, do we live?

I think the answer is to organize your laundry room. Or clean your office. Or feed your children dinner.

This sounds like nonsense, doesn't it? There's an election coming up that very well could tear this country apart. There's a pandemic raging that could take my husband, parents, or another loved one away from me. Our country is plagued by intractable problems such as abortion, human trafficking, the opioid crisis, and racism. And I'm telling you that people need to clean up their laundry rooms.

Well, not all people. But I do. Mine's a mess. It's not even really a laundry room—more of a corner in the mudroom off our kitchen. It's barely working for our family now, and what I haven't told you yet is that we may be welcoming another baby in the spring: Toby's biological sibling. It's a super high-risk pregnancy, and one hundred things could go wrong before April, so who knows what will happen. But if a new baby shows up, I need my laundry room to function better. My family needs my laundry room to function better, too, if for no other reason than it's making me insane, and an insane Mama is not a good Mama.

The Venerable Catherine Doherty, who was herself a wife and mother, wrote about the importance of doing "the duty of the moment," and that's what my laundry room is for me. It's my duty of the moment. It's part of the work that Jesus has given me, at this moment in time, as a wife and mother. I am the maker of this home. And feeding my people, clothing my people, and preventing babies from pulling laundry racks down on top of themselves aren't just items for me to check off on a to-do list; they're my path to holiness. Doherty went on to explain:

> The duty of the moment is what you should be doing at any given time, in whatever place God has put you. You may not have Christ in a home-less person at your door, but you may have a little child. If you have a child, your duty of the moment may be to change a dirty diaper. So you do it. But you don't just change that diaper, you change it to the best of your ability, with great love for both God and that child. . . . There are all kinds of good Catholic things you can do, but whatever they are, you have to realize that there is always the duty of the moment to be done. And it must be done, because the duty of the moment is the duty of God.[25]

Your duty of the moment is different than mine. You could have a roommate come home this evening who is upset about a breakup. If so, then the duty Jesus is present-ing to you in this moment is to listen to your roommate. And not to half listen to her while you wait to talk about your own day, but to give her your undivided and loving attention, as if you were listening to Christ Himself.

Or maybe you're planning a conference at work. If so, instead of wasting time online waiting for Jonah Goldberg to post his latest story on the Florida recount, make the phone call to the hotel to confirm the number of reservations that have been made and get the menu to the caterer. Those are your duties of the moment, which you need to do like you are planning that conference for Jesus Christ.

One of the reasons the world has gone so mad is because many of us aren't doing the duty of the moment. Instead of playing with our children or taking a meal to a new mom or reading the book for class or mowing our yard, we're arguing with strangers online. We're not loving the person in front of us; we're berating some person who lives 1800 miles away and whom we've never met in real life. We're fretting about the faults of people we don't know, about problems we can't control, about things we don't understand, and we're neglecting to do the work Jesus has asked us to do for Him, in the present moment, with the people who are right in front of us.

That's not a way to live. It's not a good way to prepare for death either. The saints are clear on this one. Along with Catherine Doherty, there is a veritable chorus of them singing the praises of growing in holiness by simply doing your present duty with love, from St. Thérèse of Lisieux and her "little way" to Venerable Fulton Sheen, who taught that "motive is what makes the saint." He continued:

> The typist at the desk working on routine letters, the street cleaner with his broom, the farmer tilling the field with his horses, the doctor bending over the patient, the lawyer trying a case, the student with his books, the sick in their isolation and pain, the teacher drilling her pupils, the mother dressing

the children—every such task, every such duty, can be ennobled and spiritualized if it is done in God's name."[26]

There is a time and a place for thinking about the problems of the world. There is a time and a place for voting and marching and discussing current events with friends. At times, those are the duty of the moment. But most of the time, it's washing the dishes, paying your bills, or calling your mother. It's fulfilling the duties of your vocation, whether as a single woman or a married mother of two with another on the way.

Focus on the duty of the moment, Emily. When life feels out of control, when the world seems to be breaking apart, when worries about the future consume you and you feel like there's nothing you can do to make a difference, focus on what's immediately in front of you. Do the duty of the moment. Do your work. Love your people. Change what you can. Invest your time and your energy in the responsibilities God has entrusted to you, not the ones He hasn't. See Jesus in Becket as you wipe his bottom and Toby as you dress him for the day and Chris as you send him off to work and your neighbor as you wave hello. Be fully present, fully attentive, fully aware, doing everything you do for Jesus Christ.

In the end, God and the world are both better served by you organizing your laundry room, with great attention and great love, than by you fretting about people and things you can't control. And when you live like that, serving in each moment, loving in each moment, thinking of Christ in each moment, my guess is that death becomes just another moment—a moment where you do your duty and go home to the One who loves you.

Blessings,
Emily

"SUFFER WITH LOVE."

October 21, 2020
Hawthorne House

Dear Emily,

It's been a good week here. Life is finally calming down, and I'm settling into a good routine with Toby and Becket. It helps that Becket's acid reflux has improved somewhat. It helps even more than he is finally starting to sleep through the night. He is becoming the sweetest, happiest, most gorgeous little guy. I wish you could see him. You will someday. And you will love him. He's such a gift. Not just to us, but to the world.

Like Toby, though, Becket is a gift that came from great suffering. Both their birth mothers suffered through so much to give them life. And we suffered to be able to welcome them into our life. That's how it is with so many gifts. The most valuable things in life are usually born of suffering. The older you'll get, the more you'll come to understand this.

Suffering is actually what I want to talk about today. In some ways, I've been talking about it this whole time, but there's more to flesh out, especially in light of the Last Things I mentioned a couple days ago. Death, Judgement, Heaven, and Hell come at the end. But suffering comes first. It prepares us to face those Last Things. It readies us for the end.

I'm not ready to face any of that. But I have suffered. You will suffer. Not as much as many. Some days, you will look at the suffering others are enduring and wonder how they still stand. Your own suffering will seem so small by comparison. It's best not to compare crosses, though. The only way to know the weight of a cross is to carry it. And your crosses, small as they seem, will feel heavy enough to you.

Those crosses will come in many forms. You will be rejected by people you love. You will feel unwanted, unlovable, alone. You will be misunderstood, unjustly attacked, unfairly maligned. Your body will be cut open a half dozen times—to remove tumors and endometriosis and one particularly weird growth in your ear that is about to eat into your brain stem. Your body, as it turns out, likes to grow everything but a baby. You will lose people you love. Stress, fear, and worry will rob you of the peace Jesus tries to give you. And guilt will chase you through it all, shaming you for your sadness and weakness, reminding you of how much you've been given, demanding you do more.

This is not what you expected from life, is it? You want your happily ever after—prayers answered, goals met, dreams fulfilled—not suffering. Those are normal things to want. It takes a lot more maturity and holiness than either you have in the year 2000 or I have in the year 2020 to want to suffer. Suffering, the Church teaches, is not evil. But it is an encounter with evil. It is experiencing the absence of a good for which we were made: love, life, justice, peace. And that's not fun for anyone.

Standing where I am now, in the middle of life, I know enough to realize that more suffering awaits me. I have my answered prayers. I hold them in my arms every night. But I know more sorrow lies ahead. There can be no lasting happily ever after for anyone in this broken world. Jesus told us, "In the world you have tribulation" (John 16:33). I trust I'm not the exception.

I also trust, however, that Jesus meant what He said next: "Be of good cheer, I have overcome the world" (16:34). Because of Him, I have hope that at the end of this life, I will get my happily ever after. I have faith that I will find that everlasting joy in Jesus, when at long last, I get to see His face. I also trust that all the suffering behind me and all the suffering ahead of me will help get me to that moment.

I think that's the difference between where I am now at forty-five and where you are at twenty-five. I'm still scared of suffering. I don't want to suffer. But I am grateful I have suffered. And I believe I will be grateful again for the suffering to come.

The holy French priest St. John Vianney once wrote, "There are two ways to suffer: to suffer with love and to suffer without love."

To suffer without love, he explained, is to resent the crosses God permits to come our way. It is to fear them, run from them when we can, and reject them if we can. When we reject those crosses, though, we don't get a cross-free existence. Other crosses come that are heavier and more unwieldly than the ones first rejected.

To suffer with love, however, is to recognize that through suffering, God draws us closer to Himself. Through our limitations and weaknesses, He reminds us of our need for Him. He teaches us trust, patience, and perseverance. He purifies us and prepares us to enter into an eternity with

Him. This is why St. Thérèse of Lisieux could write, "Suffering is the very best gift [God] has to give us."

This is possible because of Jesus. On the cross, He suffered, and on the cross, He loved. He suffered perfectly. He loved perfectly. And His love transformed His suffering. It made it redemptive. It made it salvific. But it didn't just transform His suffering. It transformed suffering itself. It's like Jesus's love for the Father and for us filled up the cup of His pain past the point of overflowing. He had so much love that it spilled over, running out into the world, transcending space and time to touch and transform the pain of all those who united themselves to Him, making our suffering redemptive, too.

As I wrote earlier, St. Paul tells us that our sufferings "complete what is lacking in Christ's afflictions for the sake of his body, that is, the Church" (Col 1:24). When we suffer with love—when we suffer with Christ who is Love—our sorrows become the means by which evil is overcome—evil in the world and evil in us.

When you choose to suffer with love, Emily, you become a far better woman. The crosses you carry will soften your hardest edges. They will humble you and gentle you. You will have more compassion and more love for others because of your suffering. You will become slower to judge, quicker to forgive, more hesitant to shoot from the hip. You still will shoot from the hip. Just not as often.

During the seasons of loneliness and longing that await you, run to Calvary in your heart. Seek out Jesus on the cross, rejected by those He came to save, and keep Him company. When your temper or your anxiety or some other weakness gets the better of you, close your eyes and imagine yourself kneeling beneath the cross, hiding at His feet. And when life isn't fair, when persecutions and injustice come your way, imagine your hands resting beneath our Lord's as nails pierce through them, first His hands, then yours, binding you to Him through those wounds.

On Calvary, with Jesus, you will feel His mercy. Christ's compassion, love, and courage will wash over you in your hours of greatest grief. And like the good thief, who hung beside Him, you will be changed.

It's suffering, Emily, that will lead you to where I am now. The husband I love, the babies I adore, the life we lead together, would not be mine if I hadn't walked with Jesus through the Valley of Tears, trying not to run, trying not to take the world's way out. Because the world did offer me a way out. From loneliness. From singleness. From infertility. From injustice.

But somehow, by God's grace, I said no to the world and yes to Christ. And even though the crosses I carried felt heavy, that pain, born with love, led me here, to this blessed now. That's why I trust that the pain still to come, if also born with love, will lead me home. When we suffer with love, we suffer with the One who is Love, and He shows us the way. He is the way.

For now, don't spend too much time worrying about the suffering ahead. You're not being given the grace to deal with it yet. Just hold fast to Jesus as you carry your present cross. Receive the grace He is offering you now. And trust that as new crosses come, new graces will come, too: new graces to love, new graces to believe, new graces to face whatever lies ahead with courage. Know that Christ is with you. Keep your eyes on Him. And He will use your suffering. Not just to change you. But to change this whole wayward world.

Death comes at the end. But suffering comes first. Thank God for that.

Blessings,
Emily

·᠊ᢙᡃᢒ·

43

"PRAY FOR HOPE."

October 26, 2020
Hawthorne House

Dear Emily,

A woman whom I know and respect greatly is dying. She is a beautiful woman, inside and out. She has beautiful children, some with very special needs. She has a faithful, loving husband, who adores her. She has so much living left to do, and when I heard the news about her cancer, I had words for God.

"How could you?" I reproached Him. "Why her? Her family needs her. How are they supposed to do this without her?"

"Do you think you love her and her family more than I do?" was His immediate reply.

I shut up. Because of course He does. He loves her and him and all their beautiful babies infinitely more than I do. And He will take care of them no matter what. He sees all. He knows all. He understands what is best—not just temporarily best, but eternally best for each of us—and He moves mountains to clear the path for us to get to that best. We can still choose what's not the best. We can attempt to thwart Him at every turning point. But He doesn't give up. Not until the very end, when our decisions are set, and our final choice—for Him or against Him—is set like cement in our hearts.

Occasionally, I'm afraid of death. The unknown is still not a favorite of mine. But I'm more afraid of that cement. I'm afraid of standing before Jesus and finding that my heart has become so hardened around some certain sin that I won't be able to give it to Jesus. That I will choose to keep my whole heart rather than give up the sin that's embedded in it.

But then I think of Jesus's face—His beautiful, merciful face—and my hope returns.

Hope is what makes all the difference when you are standing where I am, Emily, in a world full of dying, looking forward at Heaven and Hell. Most people dread the dying. By and large, we do everything we can to avoid it. Which we can't. Not a one of us. Sooner or later, we all have to walk through that door, which will take us either home, to Heaven, to the life and the place for which we were made, or to Hell, which is as far away from home as anyone can possibly go.

That's why death is not really the thing to fear. What we should fear is ourselves. Our self-love. Our pride. Our vanity. Our attachment to the things of the world—even the good things. All of it can become the cement that hardens our hearts and leads us to choose self over Christ, Hell over Heaven.

Hope, however, can prevent that.

The hope I'm talking about isn't the world's hope. It's not wishful thinking or some kind of cheery optimism that believes everything in life will go our way. Rather, this hope is supernatural hope, which is hope that comes from God.

The Church calls this hope a theological virtue, and like the other theological virtues (faith and charity), it's a grace that readies our souls for Heaven and prepares our hearts for eternal life. Hope in particular does that by helping us keep our priorities straight.

Faith tells you what choices to make in life, what choices will lead you to Heaven and what choices will lead you to Hell. Charity, or love, animates our good choices, calling us away from self-love and toward the love of God and neighbor. But hope is what keeps you choosing the good, over and over again, even when it's hard, even when you're scared, even when you know it could cost you everything. Hope keeps you saying yes to God's ways and no to the world's ways, until you're all the way home. Hope is what gives you the desire to choose God at all. Hope is the desire for Heaven. Which is to say, hope is the desire to be with Jesus.

By now, you should know Satan is relentless. He wants sin to take root in your heart. He wants it to plant itself so deeply that faith and charity cannot eradicate it. Over the course of your life, to make this happen, he will throw approximately nine billion temptations your way. He will tempt you to cheat, to lie, to gossip; to use someone, mislead someone, abandon someone; to give yourself over to envy, pride, wrath, lust, greed, jealousy, and gluttony; to break commitments, compromise beliefs, ignore responsibilities; to pursue things that don't matter and ignore things that do; to drown in self-pity; and through it all, to reject truth, reject Church teaching, reject Christ.

In the years to come, Emily, you will be tempted to doubt God's goodness and the goodness of His will. You will wonder if He really loves you and if there's any point to following His commandments. You will also wonder if perhaps you would be happier doing what the world says will make you happy and not what the Church says will make you happy. You will look around you, at all the good things that fill your home and the earth, and think that perhaps this, what you have and can hold, is better than what lies beyond the veil, hidden and uncertain.

Hope is what helps you navigate that minefield. As the *Catechism* explains it, "Hope is the theological virtue by which we desire the kingdom of heaven and eternal life as our happiness, placing our trust in Christ's promises and relying not on our own strength, but on the help of the grace of the Holy Spirit" (1817).

In other words, hope reminds you what matters most and Who matters most. Hope keeps your eyes fixed on Jesus and your feet fixed on the path to which He's called you. Hope helps you choose His will and His ways and, above all, Him, so you can reject the seeds of sin trying to take root in your heart and cling to Jesus's promise of life everlasting.

You will need hope every day of your life, Emily, but you especially will need it now, where I am, at the end of the world. You need to desire the life to come more than you desire this life now. You need to value the life of God in your soul more than you desire the life of your body. If not, you will cling to this life at the cost of your soul. You will reject the nourishment God wants to give you. You will neglect those who need you. You will come to see people as vectors of disease, not images of God, and you will treat them as such.

Life without hope is no life at all. It is to begin living in hell, while still on earth.

So, how do you get hope?

Unlike the cardinal virtues—prudence, justice, fortitude, temperance—you can't work at growing in hope. Those virtues are human virtues, good habits, which you build through effort and practice. But hope, like faith and charity, is a gift from God. It's given in Baptism, then strengthened by the other sacraments, with the desire for life with God increasing as the life of God grows within us. Every time you receive the Eucharist worthily or go Confession or receive the Anointing of the Sick, greater hope is poured into your soul. God also loves to give good gifts to His children, and prayers for greater hope, like greater faith and greater charity, never go unanswered.

So, pray for hope. Ask Jesus to remind you that He satisfies, that He doesn't disappoint, that He is enough, always and forever. Beg Him for the grace to care more about Him, His will, and His life, than you care about yourself, your will, and your life. If you do, then when the last day comes and you stand before Him, face to face, there will be no more choices for you to make because your heart will already be His, not hardened with sin, but alive with love. And you can go home.

Blessings,
Emily

"DON'T PUT WORKS OF WONDER IN A BOX."

October 29, 2020
Hawthorne House

Dear Emily,

About a year from your now, on a cold November night in 2001, God will give you a great gift. It's not a unique gift. You find out eventually He's given it to others. But on this occasion, it was for you. And it was holy.

On that night, you will be sitting where I always imagine you reading these letters—in the old Xandos coffee shop on Pennsylvania Avenue, on the second floor, in your favorite booth, the one near the back. On this particular night, you're reading T. S. Eliot's *Four Quartets*. At some point, you look up and glance around. Only a few other people are there that night: a middle-aged couple sipping coffee; the Ethiopian waitress from the bagel shop by your office; that grad student who is always there, writing or studying; and an older man, eating alone.

One second, they look ordinary, unremarkable. The next, they are luminous. Each is more radiant than a polished diamond. Each is bathed in a light that looks like love. And somehow, in that light, you see them—not their wrinkles or their worries or their sins, but them, the persons God created them to be. They're perfect. Precious. Sacred.

The beloved masterpiece of the Father, made in His image. In that moment, you want to bow down before them. Or hold their hands, kiss their faces, and throw your arms around them. They are so beautiful, so loved. You want them to know you see that. And you want them to see it, too. Instead, you weep.

Then everything is ordinary again. But nothing is the same.

Nineteen years have passed since that night, Emily, and not once since then have I questioned why Jesus died for us. I've also not questioned why Satan hates us. He wanted that glory all for himself, but God shared it with man. Satan's revenge is to blind us to our splendor. He doesn't want us to know how absolutely, unequivocally beloved and precious we are—each and every one of us. He doesn't want us to see it. So, he confuses us. He whispers lies to us. And he encourages us to divide, segregate, and label everyone we see, including ourselves.

Satan doesn't want you to see people. He wants you to brand people. He wants you to stamp and categorize human beings like cattle, labeling them according to their politics, theology, class, education, tax bracket, sex, skin color, ethnicity, personal sins, personal wounds, and usefulness to you. He also wants you to see yourself this way, to define yourself by one part of yourself. He doesn't want you to root your identity in the Father's love, but rather in some label you bear.

We go along with him. Because it's easy. It makes us feel safe. It gives us an identity in which we can find security. It gives us a place to belong. It also draws clear lines for us between friend and enemy, good and bad. But the ultimate result isn't safety or clarity. It's hatred. It's fragmentation, isolation, and spiritual poverty. Every great evil that afflicts our culture—abortion, racism, anti-Semitism, misogyny, human trafficking, pornography, the exploitation of workers, xenophobia—is rooted in branding people rather than seeing them as images of God.

This is the most destructive kind of evil. For when we brand ourselves, we forget who we are. We forget how much we have to offer God and each other. More tragically, when we brand others, we forget who they are. We miss out on the fullness of their beauty and their gifts. We make false assumptions about what people believe, think, and know. We allow bias and prejudice to shape our expectations. We look at a person, but we don't see them; we see their label. So, we can't love them. Nor can we learn from them. Instead, we destroy them.

Branding allows us to hate people who don't wear the same label we wear. It encourages us to blame them for what's wrong with the world. And we do. Instead of looking at each other and seeing a creature made to shine like the sun, we look at each other and see someone not as worthy as "our kind"—not as worthy of respect, not as worthy of justice, not as worthy of mercy, not as worthy of kindness, not as worthy of life.

Don't let Satan confuse you, Emily. You are not a brand. You are not your politics. You are not your wounds. You are not your past. You are not your insecurities. You are not your sins. You are not your gifts. What you are is a beloved daughter of the Father. You are the woman Jesus died to save. You too are as precious as those people you will see in the coffeeshop on that cold November night. No one thing makes you special. One thousand things make you special—your mind, your heart, your body, your heritage, your passions, your past, your present, your future. Every part of you is a gift from God to the world. The whole package matters. You are a masterpiece, with depths for others to plumb and riches for others to discover and quirks for others to tolerate. So is everyone else.

Every person you see on the street, at the office, on social media, is a complex world of loves and hates, dreams and desires, joys and hurts. Every person images God in some gorgeous and singular way. We are all unrepeatable works of wonder. And you don't put works of wonder in a box. You don't slap a label on them or brand them as just one thing. You listen to them. You contemplate them. You get to know them from every angle, appreciating every part of them, not just one.

Most of all, you love them. You die for them if need be. Because they are your brothers and sisters, who want the same things as you and fear the same things as you and bear the same image of God that abides in you. What was it James Baldwin once said?

> You think your pain and your heartbreak are unprecedented in the history of the world, but then you read. It was Dostoevsky and Dickens who taught me that the things that tormented me most were the very things that connected me with all the people who were alive, or who ever had been alive.[27]

We are all family. We all love. We all hurt. We are all bathed in the light that looks like love. Live that way. Die that way. See yourself and every person on this planet as God sees you. When you stand before Jesus, He won't see the label you've slapped on yourself or that others have slapped on you. He will see you, in all your stunning complexity. And He will love you. Rejoice in that. Be freed by that.

Blessings,
Emily

·ᴔᴑᴓ·
45

"GOD LOVES YOU."

November 2, 2020
Hawthorne House

Dear Emily,
This is the forty-fifth letter I've written you. I've written a
lot, but there's still so much I haven't told you. I've left out
the little (yet important) things, like meat tastes best rare,
the only way to make a proper martini is to put the glass
in the freezer first, and sunscreen is your friend. Also,
toilet paper. I keep meaning to mention this to you. Make
sure, sometime in February of 2020, you stock up on toilet
paper (the good stuff). Gin, too.

I also had other big things I wanted to talk about, like
how important it is to not be less Catholic or more Catholic than the Church. Also, tithe, always, even when you feel
like you have nothing to spare. Give from your poverty, not
your abundance. And get to Confession often, even when
you don't have serious sins to confess. You don't wait until
you're caked in mud and crawling with lice to take a shower,
so you shouldn't wait for Confession until your soul is in
that state either. A good clearing of the conscience every
four weeks or so will do wonders for your spiritual growth.

I wish I had time to tell you more, but I have two babies
here who need my attention, another baby still possibly on
the way, and much, much work to be done. Plus, the presi-

dential election is tomorrow. Depending on how it goes, my days for writing could be limited. What did God say? "The fire next time."

Before the fire falls, though, I want to repeat one more time the most important words you will ever hear: God loves you.

Yes, I just wrote that in my last letter. And probably in two dozen other letters. But I'm repeating it one more time, because I know how easy it is for you to tune those words out, to not take them seriously, and to not take them personally.

I know, because I was you, and I remember how often I used to do that. I would even get annoyed when people said it—when I would hear it preached in homilies or repeated in talks at conferences. "We know, we know!" I'd think. "We hear it all the time. So how about telling people something they don't know? Like, go to Confession or don't use contraception."

Then, I became a mom.

As Toby and Becket's mom, I want them to know many things. I want them to know right from wrong, good from bad, and healthy from unhealthy. I want them to know who they are and who God made them to be. More immediately, I want Toby to know he can't climb on top of the oven and I want Becket to know that tummy time is not cruel and unusual punishment.

But above all, I want my boys to know that I love them. I want them to know that I have loved them every moment of their existence. I want them to know that I think they are wonderful, precious, and glorious, not because of anything they do but simply because they are. And I want them to know that I will go on loving them, no matter how they struggle or fall or fail. I want them to know that I'll go on loving them, even if someday they tell me they don't love me back.

As for all the other stuff I want them to know? It all comes back to love. I want them to know everything else because I love them. Love comes first. The rest is rooted in love. It flows from it. It also will go down easier because of it. Love is the greatest teacher.

The more I've prayed about that desire, though, the more I understand that it doesn't come from me. It comes from God. It's a glimpse into His Fatherly heart, which longs for us to know, more than anything else, that He loves us—eternally, totally, completely.

And yes, God too wants us to know more than just His love. He wants us to know truth and goodness and beauty. He wants us to know Him. But He wants that for us because He loves us. No matter how many times we fail. No matter how much we fight against Him. No matter how often we try to run away from Him. He loves us. He loves you, personally, individually, specifically—and infinitely more than I love Toby or Becket.

If you were to die tomorrow, His love is what God would most want you to die knowing. More than the *Summa*. More than the *Catechism*. His love. That's what He wants you to know. That's what He wants you to choose. And He will give you every possible chance, until the very last moment your soul lingers in this world, to believe that He loves you and to choose His love. He will give you every possible chance to choose Him.

Once that last moment passes, though, the time for

choosing is done. You will have made your decision: Him or Not Him. Don't wait until then to make your choice. Choose Him today. Choose Him tomorrow. Choose Him every day, for as long as you have breath in your body.

You will never regret that choice, Emily. God knows you. God made you. He is your home. You can trust Him. You can trust that if you keep choosing Him, whatever suffering you endure will not be the end of your story. You can trust that your life will not be the sum of its sorrows. You can trust that whatever pain, loss, or failure you experience, somehow, in Jesus's hands, will be transformed. You can trust that no matter how hard life gets, no matter which of your worst fears comes to pass, that on the last day, when all is revealed, you will see that every tear you shed was worth it. That the good our God brought out of your journey is unimaginably more beautiful and glorious than the pain you endured. The pain is passing. The good is everlasting.

God knows what He is about. He will not lead you astray. He loves you. Love Himself loves you.

No one can repeat that often enough.

Blessings,
Emily

ENDNOTES

1 Faustina Kowalska, *Divine Mercy in My Soul: Diary of Saint Maria Faustina Kowalska* (Stockbridge: Marian Press, 2003), 1656.

2 Sigrid Undset, *Catherine of Siena* (San Francisco: Ignatius, 2009), 40.

3 Catherine of Siena, *The Dialogue*, trans. Suzanne Noffke, O.P. (New York: Paulist Press, 1980), no. 13, p. 48.

4 "Two Letters of St. Thérèse of Lisieux to Abbe Belliere," *Engaging Faith Blog*, Ave Maria Press, accessed February 24, 2021, https://www.avemariapress.com/engaging-faith/two-letters-st-therese-lisieux-abbe-belliere.

5 C. S. Lewis, *The Screwtape Letters* (New York: MacMillan, 1961), 3.

6 Dorothy Day, *All the Way to Heaven: The Selected Letters of Dorothy Day*, ed. Robert Ellsberg (Milwaukee: Marquette University Press, 2010), 452.

7 T. S. Eliot, "Little Gidding," in *Four Quartets* (Boston: HMH Books, 2014), 51.

8 *Compendium of the Social Doctrine of the Church* (2004), §58.

9 *Compendium*, §577.

10 St. John Eudes, *Le Cœur admirable*, quoted in Raoul Plus, S.J., "Reparation to the Sacred Heart," Catholic Tradition, accessed February 24, 2021, http://www.catholictradition.org/Two-Hearts/reparation1b.htm.

11 John Paul II, *Man and Woman He Created Them: A Theology of the Body*, trans. Michael Waldstein (Boston: Pauline Books and Media, 2006), 21:2.

12 Edith Stein, "Fundamental Principles of a Woman's

Education," in *The Collected Works of Edith Stein, Vol. 2: Essays on Women* (Washington, D.C.: ICS Publishing, 1987), 132–133.

13 Augustine of Hippo, *Genesi Ad Litteram*, trans. John H. Taylor, *Speculum* 25, no. 1 (Jan 1950): 87.

14 Thomas Aquinas, *The Summa Theologica of St. Thomas Aquinas*, trans. The Fathers of the English Dominican Province (London: Burns, Oates & Washbourne, 1920), II-II, q. 1, a. 1, s.c.

15 Lewis, *The Screwtape Letters*, 68.

16 Benedict XVI, Message for the 47th Annual World Communications Day, May 12, 2013, http://www.vatican.va/content/benedict-xvi/en/messages/communications/documents/hf_ben-xvi_mes_20130124_47th-world-communications-day.html.

17 Robert Farrar Capon, *The Supper of the Lamb: A Culinary Reflection* (New York: Random House, 1967), 17.

18 John Paul II, *Familiaris Consortio* (1981), §23.

19 John Paul II, *Familiaris Consortio*, §23.

20 G. K. Chesterton, "The Emancipation of Domesticity," in *Brave New Family* (San Francisco: Ignatius, 1990), 113.

21 John Paul II, quoted in Ralph Martin, *The Fulfillment of All Desire: A Guidebook for the Journey to God Based on the Wisdom of the Saints* (Steubenville, OH: Emmaus Road, 2006), 129.

22 Francis de Sales, *Introduction to the Devout Life* (New York: Catholic Book Publishing Company, 1946) 111.

23 Francis de Sales, *Introduction to the Devout Life*, 119.

24 Undset, *Catherine of Siena*, 46.

25 Catherine Doherty, "The Duty of the Moment," in *Dear Parents: A Gift of Love for Families* (Combermere, ON:

Madonna House Publications, 1997), 61.

26 Fulton Sheen, "Sanctifying the Moment," in *Lift up Your Heart: A Guide to Spiritual Peace* (Ann Arbor, MI: Liguori Publications, 2009), 214.

27 James Baldwin, quoted in an interview with Jane Howard, "Doom and Glory of Knowing Who You Are," *Life Magazine*, May 24, 1963, 89.